RE-IMAGINING PHILANTHROPY

charities need your mind more than your money

RE-IMAGINING PHILANTHROPY
charities need your mind more than your money

Revised Edition - 2017

Author: Jimmy LaRose

Editor: Bishop Redfern II

Contributor: Kathleen Robinson

Contributor: Louise Slater

Cover Design: Gabe Lowe

Photography: Rob Wilson Photography

Hair & Makeup: Amanda McClain

National Development Institute, Inc.
PO Box 1840
Lexington, SC 29071

www.JimmyLaRose.com
www.NonprofitConferences.org
www.MajorGiftsRampUp.com
www.NANOE.org

Ordering Information: Quantity sales. Special discounts are available on quantity purchases by corporations, associations, and others. For details, contact the publisher at (800) 257-6670

Printed in the United States of America

Library of Congress Control Number: 2014922757
CPSIA Code: PBANG0915A
ISBN-10: 0692358013
ISBN-13: 978-0-692-35801-6
Second Edition
10 9 8 7 6 5 4 3 2

for Kristi, who taught me how to re-imagine everything

TABLES OF CONTENTS

ACKNOWLEDGEMENTS

To Kristi LaRose, my muse, who carries me and each member of our team on her shoulders lifting us up…holding us high…making sure all our dreams come true.

To Bishop Redfern II, my friend, who started each day by reading and expanding this work. I may have written this book, however, Redfern spent countless hours making it glow.

To Honnie Korngold, my cheerleader, whose vision for my life knows no bounds. She sees everything with largess and transforms all that she considers.

To Wesley Rediger, my mentor, who for three decades required me to think differently. He taught me how to re-imagine the way we could live our lives.

To Hall Powell, my example, whose life of service to family, ministry and nonprofits inspires us all. Whenever any of us have a question we always call Hall.

To Louise Slater, my encouragement, for her life-long commitment to making straight another's way. She finds needs and meets them. She does this for many, she did it for me.

To Kathleen Robinson, my professor, whose academic commitment to the nonprofit sector is without match. Her integrity and attention to my work has made it invaluable to all.

To Charlotte Berry, my volunteer, for her unwavering support of my mission and her unparalleled example of what it truly means to serve nonprofits.

To Jerry Strickland, my donor, who considered us and others when designing his own transition. I see him in the persons of Patia, Megan & Carter.

To Steven LaRose, my only brother, who through his faithfulness to friends and family has taught us all the meaning of the word "duty."

To Joseph LaRose, my father, who gave everything he had so that his sons would have more. He made my life possible.

To Sharon LaRose, my mother, from whom I derive my talent. She wrote books long before me. She's ensured I experience life worth living.

ABOUT THE AUTHOR

www.JimmyLaRose.com

Jimmy LaRose's passion for "people who give" has inspired philanthropists around the world to change the way they invest in nonprofits. His belief that donors are uniquely positioned to give charities what they truly need – leadership before finance – is the basis for his work with individuals, governments, corporations, and foundations, in the U.S., Europe, Asia and Middle East. Jimmy, in his role as author, speaker, corporate CEO and nonprofit CEO, champions all of civil society's vital causes by facilitating acts of benevolence that brings healing to humanity and advances our common good. Now, in his twenty-fifth year of service, his message that money is more important than mission and donors are more important than people or causes has resonated with policy institute scholars, social activists, doctoral students, business leaders, think tanks, nonprofit and NGO executives who rely on him and his team of veterans to meaningfully grow their charitable enterprise.

He's the architect of the Major Gifts Ramp-Up™ Donor Cultivation Model and Cloud used by charities around the world to meet the needs of their primary customers…the advocates, donors, and volunteers who financially underwrite their mission.

www.MajorGiftsRampUp.com

He's the founder of National Development Institute™, a 501(c)3 public benefit charity established in 1990 that insures funders, granting organizations, and corporations safeguard their mission by building capacity within charities who serve the human welfare, education, health care, arts and environmental sectors.

www.NonprofitConferences.org

He's the inventor of DonorScope™ a prospect research platform used by charities to identify donors who give big gifts to great dreams that are backed by sound plans.

www.DonorScope.com

He is the founder of both Development Systems International™ and PAX Global™ firms that specialize in implementing the Major Gifts Ramp-Up for nonprofits, ministries, and churches who raise major gifts.

www.Development.net & www.PAXglobal.com

Jimmy is a co-founder of the National Association of Nonprofit Organizations & Executives (NANOE). NANOE members believe that "innovation never fears a challenge" and that the greatest contribution nonprofit practitioners can make to charity is to become the creative enterprise-leaders our sector so desperately needs. NANOE is the only nationwide membership organization in the U.S. for Executives seeking credentials in the art of nonprofit capacity-building.

www.NANOE.org

James P. LaRose has served as a specialist with the U.S. State Department's Speakers Bureau traveling the world working with embassies, foreign governments, and leaders to promote philanthropy and civil society in developing countries. He was the founding President of the Western Maryland Chapter of the Association of Fundraising Professionals (AFP), and is a graduate of AFP's Faculty Training Academy (FTA). He is a graduate of Indiana University's Executive Leadership Program, Indianapolis, IN, the National Planned Giving Institute, Memphis, TN, Tennessee Temple University, Chattanooga, TN and the Word of Life Bible Institute, Schroon Lake, NY. Rev. LaRose was ordained as minister of the gospel by the Ecumenical Church of Christ in further support of his service to the hurting and hopeless around the world. He and his beautiful wife Kristi are citizens of the Palmetto State where they make their home in Lexington, South Carolina.

"Things" known to be "unchangeable" are mostly transformed via the architect whose command of the constants are rooted in the Divine.

~Jimmy LaRose

01010111 01101000 01100001 01110100 00100000 01100010 01100101 01100001 01110100 01110011 00100000 01101111 01101110 01100101 01110011 00100000 01101101 01101110 01100101 01110011 01100000 01100001 01101110 01100100 00100000 01111001 01101011 01110010 01110011 01101011 01110011 00111111 10110101 01110011 00111111

RE-IMAGINING PHILANTHROPY

THE MOTIVE

si vivendum est, bene vivant

If they must live, let them live well

~Quintus Horatius Flaccus, 65 BC

Would you indulge me for a moment?

In the pages to follow, I'll share with you a series of startling "behind the scenes" stories that reveal the truth about the current state of nonprofit management. These revelations will each be paired with bold solutions that, *with your help*, will transform the charitable sector.

Sharing stories when writing a book is the safer play. You see, regardless of what you think of my conclusions, the stories stand on their own as both accurate and real. You'll decide whether or not these provocative and entertaining accounts resonate with your own experiences, and whether or not they are important enough to share with others.

But like I said, *that's the safer play.*

What isn't safe would be to establish a premise, or (dare I say) an "axiom" that ties all these stories together.

Here's the danger.

Why read a book if it's probable that, at any point in the future, its basic premise will prove untrue?

We live during a particular moment in time, where global "shifts in consciousness" are the norm. The enduring query "What is Truth?" is no longer a matter of debate. Postmodernism has declared that nothing has ever been knowable, axiom is subject to context, and pragmatism is preferred over ethic.

(I'm not complaining. Our present state of awareness is not all that bad, if one considers the appalling damage persons armed with "dogma" have wrought on mankind. *Even more humbling is the realization that, too many times in the past, I've been part of the non-thinking mob.*)

Regardless, relativism challenges philanthropy's merit, for how can we give to a cause if the proposed "case" proves to be untrue, or will become untrue in the near or far future? Important questions like the following will remain unanswered:

> "Should I give to breast cancer research?"
> "Why volunteer at the food bank?"
> "Should I go overseas with my church?"
> "Why am I being asked to join the museum's membership circle?"
> "Should I serve on the board of the local counseling center?"
> "Why am I so passionate about saving the ocean?"

Wouldn't it be helpful, even miraculous (considering the vast array of philosophies, theologies, methodologies, and motivations shared among us), *to propose a common absolute in which we might universally trust?*

I'd like to suggest that it would be a whole lot easier to read this book if there was at least one thing we could all agree upon right from the start?

So, let us discern for ourselves that most elusive of ideas…*a common value, upon which we can build something meaningful.*

Wouldn't it be a whole lot easier to read this book if there was at least *one thing* we could all agree upon right from the start?

Here we go.

WEBSTER'S DEFINTION OF <u>AXIOM</u>

1: a maxim widely accepted on its intrinsic merit
2: an established rule or principle or a self-evident truth

Here's my proposal. Let's call it...

...MANIFEST LIVING

If a person or a thing possesses life, *it is better that, for a determinate period of time, this someone or something should be alive*, rather than dead. And that, during that finite span and inherent to their animation, there is a hierarchy of needs that, if met, dignifies the life being lived.

Therefore...   ...EXISTENCE IS GOOD...
                          ...GOOD EXISTENCE IS...

<u>**Simply put, it is a better thing that one lives, and if they live, experience a life worth living.**</u>

Today, I met a person who, from her own overflowing cup, shared a drink with another. She possesses that lethal combination of *self-awareness and abundance* that destroys destitution and fellowships another into provision's wake. She gave from what she had...not from what she didn't

15

have. It was both magnificent and startling, for, without effort, *she made another person's life worth living.*

It is a better thing that one lives and if they live, experience a *life worth living.*

Combine the concept of philanthropy with manifest living, and a richer and more accurate definition of giving emerges.

WEBSTER'S DEFINITION OF <u>PHILANTHROPY</u>

1: Phileo (Greek) kindness, benevolence, love
2: Anthropos (Greek) mankind

Philanthropy, defined as "love of mankind," when fused with Manifest Living, *produces an active benevolence, ensuring another possesses life worth living.*

All living things…man, animal, plant, fungi, protest, and moneran kingdoms…*all may apply!*

Is there any import? What's the payoff?

Here's a possible outcome.

<u>These ideas allow us to RESPECT any and all attempts, successes, and failures others employ to help another.</u> The countless ways a philanthropist contributes to another's life worth living is fraught with subjectivity. For some may believe that…

...Sharing religious beliefs improves another's life
...Saving the oceans improves another's life
...Contributing to arts and culture improves another's life
...Giving canned goods to the food bank improves another's life
...Ensuring families have access to counseling improves another's life
...Investing in breast cancer research improves another's life

Regardless of one's political persuasion, politics, theology, or method...
PHILANTHROPY combined with MANIFEST LIVING demands
appreciation for the diverse and innumerable ways *others help others*.
These thoughts, actions, and generosities are the cornerstone of a
foundation upon which civil society has been built for 4,000 years.

SO, MANIFEST LIVING AMPLIFIES PHILANTHROPY WHEN...

...out of the abundance with which I've been entrusted...

...I contribute to another person's life...

...ensuring that they, like me, experience live worth living.

For those of us who possess a life full of love and abundance, and are in
no danger of lack, let us heed the words of the wise man who said...

"I would rather have it said, 'He lived usefully,' than, 'He died rich.'"

Thank you for spending a few moments of your time with me. I look
forward to meeting you personally. I look forward to the journey we're
about to share together.

Jimmy LaRose

jimmy@jimmylarose.com

17

RE-IMAGINING PHILANTHROPY QUIZ (RIP QUIZ)

What's a RIP Quiz?

Each section of RE-IMAGINING PHILANTHROPY ends with a series of questions that will inspire you to process and internalize the "big ideas" you discover while reading this book.

Here's your first set of questions:

RIP QUIZ #1

1. Are you comfortable with the idea that it is better to give out of abundance, rather than making a gift that may cause you financial stress?

2. There are thousands of opportunities that are worthy of investment. Have you determined what you like to give to and what you don't?

3. Name five causes, issues, or charities in whom you enjoy investing.

4. Are you comfortable saying "no" to an opportunity you may not be passionate about?

5. When you make a gift beyond your alms/tithe giving, why do you give?

6. Respond to this statement, "...out of the abundance with which I've been entrusted, I contribute to another person's life, ensuring that they, like me, experience live worth living" (write down what comes to mind).

THE MOVEMENT

On the rocky and sometimes fearsome path one travels between being a 'pupil' and being a 'student,' it is essential to grasp the awesome fact that truth never fears a challenge, and to realize that we possess the liberty to challenge the existing order of things using critical analysis, and are charged with the responsibility to become the creative, thinking opinion leaders that this world so desperately needs.

~Charles Murphy

Why write to philanthropists?

It's simple. YOU ARE OUR GREAT RECOURSE!

You see, as a benefactor, foundation exec, or corporate giver, you are uniquely positioned *to challenge the existing order of things* on behalf of a failed charitable sector.

You've already worked through many of the problems that have paralyzed nonprofits, and possess the solutions that will set us all free.

There are reasons why you're prosperous and the charitable sector is not. Donors possess a treasure trove of wealth that 501(c)3 organizations urgently require. It's not your money, it's not your network…

…it's your experiences in life and enterprise that've made you a success!

Did you hear the one about the executive director of the local charity who was walking down the street and fell into a hole with walls so steep he couldn't get out?

> His consultant passes by and the guy shouts up, "Charlie, can you help me out?" The consultant says, "I can help, but it'll cost you $5,000 dollars." The guy says, "Fine," so the consultant gets out his PowerPoint and performs a two hour training, titled, "Five Ways to Get Out of Holes With Steep Walls." He then asks the guy to remind him where to send the invoice, and moves on.

> A board member, who he hasn't heard from in weeks, come along, and the guy shouts up, "Sharon, I'm down in this hole, can you help me out?" The board member says, "Sure, I know this great nonprofit consultant, he's an expert hole problem solver, I'll have him give you a call," and moves on.

> Then a donor walks by, and the guy shouts up, "Hey Jack, it's me; can you help me out?" Jack doesn't say a word, but instead jumps down into the hole. The nonprofit exec says, "What? Why'd you do that? Now we're both in trouble." Jack replies, *"Yeah, but I've been down here before, and I know the way out."*

You're the key. *You know the way out!!!*

The ***nonprofit sector*** is flaccid, and has been saddled with a century's worth of wrong-thinking ensuring it's remained a ***non-growth sector*** for nearly fifty years. Department of Commerce statistics demonstrate that charities have been stuck since 1970, hovering right around a GDP growth-rate of 2%. During that same period, philanthropists in the private sector have enjoyed unprecedented financial success, gaining a percentage of world market-share never before seen in the history of man.

Nonprofits falsely believe that more money is the answer to their problems, which is almost as silly as giving a degenerate gambler more chips. The truth is, give the average nonprofit more money, and all you'll do is keep them in the same cycle of "crazy-making" that's paralyzed them for decades.

You see, **charities need your mind more than your money!**

The challenge before us is not to ask you for more dollars, but rather to access the proven experience you possess that, when applied, will lead us out of this wilderness.

Here's the rub. All too often, you (the donor) are a big part of the problem. Why? Here's a quote from a millionaire donor who read an earlier draft of RE-IMAGIING PHILANTHROPY. She said, *"Jimmy, why is it that every time I walk into a nonprofit board meeting, I 'check at the door' all the sound business principles and practices that made me successful in the first place?"*

"Jimmy, why is it that every time I walk into a nonprofit board meeting, 'I check at the door' all the sound business principles that made me successful in the first place?"

You see, *your success is based on the application of principles that the nonprofit sector has never embraced.* RE-IMAGINING PHILANTHROPY will reveal why you've been hesitant to hold organizations accountable to the same practices that have made you profitable. It will also reveal the ways you can ensure…CHARITIES ARE TRANSFORMED!!!

I discovered early on that, when it comes to philanthropists, money chases after *ideas*, and that there will always be generous people like you who will amply support a *great dream* that's backed by a *sound plan*.

Tragically, *great dreams* backed by *sound plans* rarely present themselves.

How long has it been since you've been startled by an idea? When's the last time you discovered a great dream that took your breath away—the type of moment when you were so inspired you had to take a minute, sit down, and consider the beauty of it all?

How long? Well, here we go…

RE-IMAGINING PHILANTHROPY will inspire you to take back control of your charitable giving and use your acumen and abilities to solve multi-billion dollar problems through a re-tooled sector you've personally transformed and clothed in immense global power.

This book will inspire you to take back control of your charitable giving and use your acumen to solve multi-billion dollar problems through a re-tooled charitable sector you've personally transformed and clothed in immense global power.

The challenges we are about to confront will require us to wade into the muck, mire, and mess of people, process, and product problems (which, historically, don't respond well to intervention). The origins of these "problems" do not come from one place, but many, and so will the solutions. Our task is to define and integrate these problems' inherent complexities in a manner that ensures we defeat them.

I was recently interviewed by *The Chronicle of Philanthropy* and was asked about the state of the nonprofit sector. I simply replied, *"It's ridiculous that we're not more effective."* The article received a lot of attention, and one disgruntled academician from New York's Columbia University wrote:

> *Although it would be nice to see perfect effectiveness at all charities, to state that it is 'ridiculous that we're not more effective' presupposes that Mr. LaRose or anyone else knows just what that **elusive "effectiveness" formula** is.*

Though I'm sure it will dismay the professor, I've discovered his "ELUSIVE EFFECTIVNESS FORMULA" and with your help, will provide charities a prescription to make them whole. I've taken twenty-five years to develop, improve, and empirically demonstrate the effectiveness of this formula. *I'm pleased to share that the solution revolves around you.*

This formula will reveal itself by first deconstructing charities' maladministration of MONEY, MOTIVES, MANAGEMENT, MEANS, METHODS, & MODELS, leading to the launch of new MOVEMENT. This "movement" will release nonprofits from the weights that have beset organizations for decades. The clarity of dysfunction I will expose will startle you…motivate you…bring out the best in you…*and elicit solutions from you that will set us free.*

The clarity of the dysfunction I will expose will startle you…motivate you…bring out the best in you…and elicit solutions from you that will set us free.

Where will this journey take you? To a place where your involvement in charity will finally begin to make sense. It's going to be an adventure, and I'd like to do this with you.

Back to the state of the charitable sector for just a minute. What if I told you that, starting January 1 of next year, you were going to be tasked with overseeing $1.65 TRILLION DOLLARS ANNUALLY FOR A PERIOD OF 20 YEARS, TOTALING $33 TRILLION DOLLARS? Your charge will be to use this massive amount of money to affect global change on behalf of important causes and people in need.

You'd think you could do something big with those kinds of resources, wouldn't you?

You'd be wrong.

The nonprofit sector is led by well-meaning individuals who, each day, collectively mismanage billions of dollars. In 2012, nonprofits generated $1.65 trillion, and spent $1.57 trillion in what is arguably a failed attempt to affect global change. Furthermore, the nonprofit sector is our nation's third-largest industry (retail trade and manufacturing being first and second) and employs 10 million people who lack the requisite skills required to defeat problems of scale.

The National Center for Charitable Statistics revealed, once again, that in 2014, the charitable sector commanded 2% of gross domestic product. This report demonstrates that in spite of the huge increase in the number of charities and the many dedicated movements to encourage greater giving, sector growth is still in decline (the high for nonprofit GDP was 2.3% in the year 2000, but since that time has fallen below 2.1% [the same percentage recorded in 1971, according to "Giving USA"]).

Dan Pallotta, noted author and defender of charity, revealed during his TED Talk, named "How we think about charity is all wrong," that within the past forty years, over 45,000 for-profit companies increased revenues beyond the $50 million dollar mark, while the number of nonprofit corporations that crossed the $50 million dollar threshold *was under 150.*

For-profit enterprise 45,000…nonprofit enterprise 150?

Wow! Now get this…

Gas prices remain low, the DOW passes the 20,000 mark, the S&P 500 reaches an all-time high AND…

…*every nonprofit you know is crying that they have no money.*

How many nonprofits do you know that comprehended the magnitude of the DOW passing 20,000? What executive directors sat down with you, exhilarated with a full comprehension that their ability to affect lives was directly connected to this historic twenty-first century achievement?

I'd dare say that the answer to this rhetorical question is "none!"

The book you're about to read reveals the reasons why.

RE-IMAGINING PHILANTHROPY will take you on a wild ride into the upside-down world of nonprofit management, exposing a clarion of ill-fated thinking that will shock and amaze you. It will also demonstrate that you possess the medicine we need to heal nonprofit organizations, and that with your help, we can become the effective organizations the world so desperately needs.

Here's the good news: T.F. Hodge wrote, "Improving the human condition takes little effort; destroying it takes maximum force."

With your help…we can do this.

It's important to recognize that we're not alone in this effort. Democracy, governments, marketplace economics, entrepreneurship, and for-profit corporations provide the greater percentage of resources humanity needs to enjoy a life worth living. The public and private sectors play the larger role in advancing causes and improving quality of life. Case in point…it's probable that you and I are less dependent on the charitable sector, and rely more on the private and public sectors for our well-being.

For instance, did you know that last year, one organization provided 40,000 hip-replacement surgeries to seniors in need? Its name is the U.S. Department of Health and Human Services (**public sector**). Another group provided 800,000 citizens living in third-world countries access to affordable cell phone service. This group calls themselves Samsung (**private sector**). Finally, another cohort is on the cusp of eradicating cancer through the creation of Delta-24-RGD, a virus that eats the same cancer cells that have killed millions. They're named MD Anderson Cancer Center (**nonprofit sector**), and are funded by the federal government (public sector), corporate gifts (private sector), and research charities (nonprofit sector).

You see, the rising tide of civil society raises all ships when interconnectivity between charities, corporations, and governments creates new business ecosystems that benefit all.

Regardless, there will always be those 20% of people who the public and private sectors will miss. *These people are dying, or worse, have no capacity to live a life worth living without you, me, and our $1.65 trillion.* Without us, they have no hope. We need to solve these problems, and I assure you we can.

Let me circle back around and tell you a little more about your role.

I was in a meeting a few weeks ago with Rusty Griffin, the patriarch of the Griffin Family Foundation in Valdosta. It was a beautiful warm Georgia afternoon, and Rusty invited us to join him and his son-in-law, Thomas Olsen, on the back patio of the "barn." We each sat down in our own rocking chair; there was a bit of a breeze, and when he offered me glass of lemonade, I couldn't help but think I'd been transported back into some sort of antebellum scene from *Gone with the Wind*.

We were discussing capacity-building and the problems that ail the charitable sector, when Rusty made the following observation.

> *"Jimmy, person after person, nonprofit after nonprofit, sits right here in these same chairs, hopeful that we'll give them a gift. They all come believing that they need our money, when what they really need…is our advice!"*

RE-IMAGINING PHILANTHROPY will teach you how to restrict the investments you give to nonprofits. ***From now on, the monies you give will be accompanied by your personal direction, and will transform charity into an effective enterprise sector to affect global change.***

In order to do this, we'll have to pull off all the scabs and take a thoughtful look at all the different issues that have paralyzed nonprofits. It won't be pretty, and the amount of pushback we'll receive may cause us to doubt our direction. I will not be guilty of throwing stones for the sake of throwing stones. No one gets any points for pulling back the curtain and pointing a finger. After all, wasn't it a dog who's credited with exposing the Wizard? The forerunner to Captain Obvious had to be the kid who blurted out, "The emperor has no clothes." What the poor guy really needed was a coat, *not a press announcement made by an infant.*

The experience you're about to have is not only provocative (see chapter title nine, *"Volunteer boards don't work and never will"*), but, more importantly, will provide you with answers that make sense, e.g., *the need to impress upon charities that the philanthropist is the true customer of nonprofits (not the people or causes being served that have no money).*

What follows will resonate with you, because you've already applied these principles in your own life and business. Combine these experiences with the influence you wield as a financial supporter, and you'll discover that you're our best hope for transformation.

Another way to look at the importance of your role would be to consider the ability of an executive director to get this book into the hands of a board member. Even if they had the courage (see chapter title fourteen, *"Nonprofits don't need Executive Directors [they need CEOs]"*), they'd have to secretly mail it to a trustee's home in a plain craft envelope without a return address.

To better support you each section of this book begins by tackling a management controversy, is illustrated by a story and then supported by a detailed alternative. *The "alternatives" provided are so comprehensive that at different moments you may find yourself transitioning from a light read into a type of reference volume. <u>Simply put, you'll find everything you need (and everything a nonprofit needs) to get started in the pages to follow.</u>*

Each section of this book…

…tackles a management controversy,

…is illustrated by a story,

…then supported by a detailed alternative,

…and ends with a quiz.

Finally (and of utmost importance), the solutions provided in the following pages are based on clinical research undertaken by Clemson

University and National Development Institute, as overseen by Dr. Kathleen Robinson and supported by the author of this book. We were privileged to perform statistical studies with over 470 nonprofit executive directors as a basis for the *"Nonprofit Capacity Building in a Post-Recession Economy."*

So, here we go! It's only going to take one person and *it could be you*. I'm already inspired by your courage, and though at first you may be viewed as far-reaching, it won't take long before hundreds of thousands of your peers join you in this groundbreaking movement.

The opportunity to lead us lies before you. I will be the first to follow.

*Please email jimmy@jimmylarose.com for a thirty page executive summary of NONPROFIT CAPACITY BUILDING IN A POST RECESSION ECONOMY

RIP QUIZ #2

1. Respond to this statement: "Nonprofits need your wisdom, as well as your cash!"

2. Are you presently investing in a nonprofit that requires significant improvements to be effective?

3. If you answered yes to the question above, can you identify what's wrong with the organization? Write down three things you know are out of order.

4. What wisdom do you have to offer nonprofits? Write down the expertise(s) you could share that transform the way they operate.

5. Name three business principles that you (or others) employ that nonprofits need to implement.

THE MONEY

There are few sorrows, however poignant,
in which a good income is of no avail

~Logan Pearsall Smith

I've been getting in a lot of trouble lately for a recent declaration I made to a group of nonprofit executives and board members. I emphatically stated,

"MONEY IS MORE IMPORTANT THAN MISSION (OR MINISTRY)"

The old adage, *there are things in life that are more important than money,* is about as silly as saying *there are things in life that are more important than air.*

Money, like air, in and of itself is not very impressive, nor does it give life meaning. However, life has very little meaning...*if you can't breathe!*

Money, Money, Money, Money.

Upon sharing this controversial axiom, many of the executives in the room pushed back, so I advised,

"Ok, let's pause and take a deep breath...Oh I'm sorry...you can't breathe?

That's because YOU GOT NO MONEY!!!"

Money is oxygen. Without it, charities asphyxiate, atrophy and fail.

It's simply a matter of THE ORDER OF THINGS. The healthy flow of lots of money (air) allows a nonprofit to flourish and, in turn, realize its important mission in ways never dreamed possible.

In case I wasn't clear, the entire nonprofit sector is all and only about money (ever think about the word "NONPROFIT?" *EVEN OUR BRAND NAME IS ABOUT MONEY.*).

Here are the facts...

The designation 501(c)3 (please note that those of us who refer to ourselves as 501(c)3 are, again, using a term about taxes, i.e. money) allows nonprofit enterprise to secure contributed revenue and in turn offer donors a tax deduction for the purpose of advancing education, health, human welfare, religion, the arts, and environment. In short, the nonprofit sector is a largely unregulated mechanism used voluntarily by individuals, corporations, and governments to direct MONIES to causes, groups and movements ensuring that others live a life worth living.

Broadly, the financial sources available to a charitable organization fall into four categories:

1. Public Funding   3. Retail Sales
2. Philanthropy   4. Fees/Tuition

Why then would you hire

...a medical doctor to head up a hospital?
...a therapist to oversee a counseling center?
...a social worker to head up child abuse prevention?
...or an educator to provost a college?

Unless they were expert CEOs with a proven record of making money for the bottom line, using marketplace economics (fees/tuition), social enterprise (retail sales), fundraising (philanthropy) or government grants (public funding). Simply put, strong nonprofits replace "do-gooders" with aggressive entrepreneurial money-making CEOs who can grow their enterprise!

Strong nonprofits replace "do-gooders" with aggressive entrepreneurial money-making CEOs who can grow their enterprise!

SMART NONPROFITS FIRE THIER EXECUTIVE DIRECTOR AND HIRE A CEO

Let me bring this home for you. What's your view of the CEO of your favorite nonprofit? Are they experts in generating fees, sales, fundraising, or grant income? Do they have a history of stabilizing organizations through sound financial management and increased revenue generation? If they don't, let them go and hire someone who does.

Why so harsh? *Because expert CEOs increase revenues to undewrite more salaries for therapists, social workers and educators, etc. who in turn ensure people in need experience a life truly worth living!*

Expert CEOs increase revenues to fund more salaries for doctors, therapists, social workers, and educators, who ensure people in need experience a life worth living!

Now, let's go further. If money is more important than mission, then...

DONORS ARE MORE IMPORTANT THAN CAUSES OR PEOPLE

To give away money is an easy matter and in any man's power.
But to decide to whom to give it and how large and when, and for
what purpose, is neither in every man's power nor an easy matter.

~Aristotle 360 B.C.

Too often (quite often), we reduce donors to ATM machines that
reside somewhere outside the organization, who we wouldn't visit or
communicate with if we didn't have to.

You see, it's much easier to be in a for-profit enterprise than a nonprofit
one. I'm reminded of author Jim Collins, who wrote, "Regarding the
social sectors, unfortunately, there is no guarantee between exceptional
results and sustained access to resources."

The for-profit business owner provides a service or a product that
customers purchase, generating income that, when properly managed,
ensures the business expands, grows, and flourishes. *Conversely, in*
nonprofit enterprise, the customer (student, homeless, rainforest, family,
etc.) historically doesn't pay for the service or product provided.

Every time I read that last line, I'm startled by how idiotic it sounds.
Tragically, it's a maxim so widely-held that few comprehend the flawed
concept in which it's rooted. Let me share it again.

Conversely, in nonprofit enterprise, the customer (student, homeless,
rainforest, family, etc.) historically doesn't pay for the service or product
provided.

You see, the premise is all wrong. Nonprofits mistakenly think that the student, homeless, rainforest, family, etc. are their customers. Your clients or causes are not customers...they got no money.

Successful nonprofits understand that donors are the object of their mission, and must be served before people in need.

DONORS ARE YOUR CUSTOMERS. Donors pay for the opportunity to participate in the transformation of a people...they underwrite the advancement of an important issue...they purchase a stake in your meaningful cause.

I received an email this morning from a precious guy who was kind enough to take the time to challenge one of my recent articles. He is the executive director of a nonprofit in the Northwest that provides vital services to women. I was writing about organizations who trick themselves into thinking that financial supporters will respond to a hired third-party who purports that they can perform the donor cultivation that nonprofits can only do themselves.

Here's what he wrote,

> Jimmy,
>
> It is interesting to me that you state that, "Nonprofits would rather avoid the hard work of donor cultivation by paying an out-of-town third party to perform the visits they should really be doing themselves."
>
> As a nonprofit director, you hit on just part of the issue. The reality is that nonprofits want to be about the work of carrying out their mission. Funding is a necessary part of that equation. It seems that, for many nonprofits, raising funds has replaced the real mission.

Nonprofits want to stay "on mission" – raising funds is a means to that end. We already do so much hard work, donor cultivation is just one slice of many responsibilities. Is it any wonder that nonprofits attempt to outsource donor cultivation?

Small organizations cannot give enough of themselves to the actual mission because of the demands of donor cultivation.

Just my two-cents. Thanks for taking the time to hear me out.

Scott

Though I don't know Scott personally, I was struck by his sincerity and kind tone. He and his team are the reason why I've spent my entire adult life in the nonprofit sector. You see, we've all been privileged to work with leaders like Scott who are simply…the finest people in the world.

Regardless, the numbers of ways Scott is wrong are countless. What's worse is his well-written, reasonable response is tragically representative of the way a majority of executive directors and board members think.

Let me make this practical. How many mission statements have you read that include you (the donor) in their narrative?

Here's a typical mission statement:

> *Harvest Town Food Bank exists to provide our community's hurting, hungry, and homeless the clothing, food, and nutritional care they so desperately need.*

Typical, isn't it?

Now, let me share with you a proper one:

Harvest Town Food Bank provides donors, volunteers, and advocates the organization they require to serve our community's hurting, hungry, and homeless.

Strong charities exist to serve donors BEFORE causes or people in need.

Strong charities exist to serve donors BEFORE causes or people in need.

When the nonprofit in whom you're investing understand this, *everything changes*…the way it operates, the way it spends monies, the way it allocates resources, *even its name!*

Here's an example. There's a spectacular charity in one of our Southern towns that supports and provides for women, children, and teens who have been ravaged by the horror of rape.

It's named Tri-State Rape Crisis and Sexual Trauma Center* (TSRCSTC).

The executive director and board of TSRCSTC attended National Development Institute's Major Gifts Ramp-Up Conference, where they were asked the question, "Who is your customer?". It basically came down to one of two groups: *women, children, and teens in crisis with no money, or donors with finances who care about people who've been hurt.*

This led to a "sacred cow" discussion around a possible name change, and whether or not their current brand worked for the organization and the community they served.

Those against altering the name were adamant. "If we water down our name, we're watering down the dreadfulness of this crime. We can't

*names have been changed to protect confidentiality

compromise." One person declared, "We must keep the ugliness of rape front and center in the minds of our citizens. Besides, those who need our services are able to access them more readily because our name clearly tells the public what we're about."

Though I understood their passion, *they were passionately wrong*. You see, ***it's not about the ugliness of rape, but rather the beauty of how this group lovingly supports people in need.***

Major League Baseball had one of their AAA farm teams in this town, and had built an amazing ballpark. During each game, it donated a portion of ticket sales to a local nonprofit. Families from all over the region brought their kids to experience America's favorite pastime. Each year, the owners gave a significant annual gift to this organization, but were NOT comfortable having a *Tri-State Rape Crisis and Sexual Trauma Center Day* to raise additional funds from their fans.

Simply put, the question "Mommy, what's rape?" was not the type of query these business owners wanted raised while entertaining families in their facility.

In another instance, a major car manufacturer who employed over 1,000 workers made a decision not to share a gift with TSRCSTC. You see, any time they made a charitable investment, they also purchased a major billboard announcing their support of that particular nonprofit. Simply put, they didn't feel it was wise to have the terms "rape" and "trauma" blazoned on a sign that also contained their brand.

The center's executive director (after attending one of our National Development Institute events) invited me to help them tackle this issue. I met with thirteen different staff, board members, and administrators around their conference room, and started by asking them to take a leap, and, for the sake of this exercise, agree that donors, not their clients, were their actual customers.

They nodded their heads, so I asked the group…

"Who are our customers?"

Someone bravely said, *"Donors are our customers."*

Pressing on, I asked, "Ok, if donors are our customers, what do they buy from us? Is it a product or service?"

The executive director thoughtfully replied, *"It's neither a product nor a service…*

…they pay for an experience."

"What type of experience?" I asked.

She replied, *"Donors to our organization share their kindness with others and are loved in return."*

(That was some higher-level thought. There was a collective gasp, followed by a big group "wow", indicating agreement.)

"Okay, who do they love?" I inquired. She answered, *"Women, children, and teens."*

I countered, "Be more specific." She expanded, "Women, children, and teens who've been abused."

I countered again, "Be more specific."

She took a second or two, and then replied,

"Okay…her name is Cassandra Duncan."

"Who?" I asked. *"Cassandra Duncan,"* she replied.

"Who's Cassandra Duncan?"

With a measure of satisfaction in her voice, she replied...

"Cassandra was the first person to walk through our doors, April 9, 1972."

"Wow...tell us about Cassandra."

The ED stood up, walked to the head of the table (inviting me to move out of her way), and began sharing:

> *Cassandra was thirty-three years old, and had been sexually abused by a playmate's father between the ages of nine and twelve. She was stable when we first met her, despite the fact that she had never told a soul about her childhood trauma. She came to us because she feared her abuser (who was still alive, twenty years later) might have still been active in the neighborhood where she grew-up. She wanted to do the right thing, but needed guidance as she faced this emotional challenge. After months of work with the center's counseling cohort, Cassandra navigated many complex obstacles, shared the truth with her family, and worked with law-enforcement to confront her abuser.*
>
> *She took a step that not only secured healing for her own wounded heart, but she protected her community as well.*
>
> *That was just the beginning. Cassandra began volunteering at the center, and made herself available to other women who needed to know they were not alone. She became active in and eventually led a weekly Life's Worth Living Group, providing women a safe place to process their experiences. In 1977, Cassandra was interviewed by both local newspaper and television, and was instrumental in raising the level of*

visibility of the realities of child abuse and rape in our community.
She agreed to share her story at fundraising events, and even partnered
with the board chair to visit a large manufacturing corporation. The
corporation's owners gave the center their largest financial gift ever.
Finally, in 1996, Cassandra joined the board of directors, and after
thirty years of service to both women and her community, she passed
away in June of 2012 at the age of seventy-three.

There was silence, and then another "WOW!"

I jumped back in, "Now remember, we started this exercise based on
the premise that supporters are your primary customers. So, would it be
fair to say you empower donors to love, care, and support women like
Cassandra?"

The executive director said, "Everyone loved Cassandra…especially our
supporters."

The board chair (who hadn't said a word all morning), matter-of-factly
chimed in with…

"Ok, let's call ourselves the *Cassandra Duncan Support Center.*"

There were startled looks around the room. The silence broke when the
executive director quietly (yet existentially) said…

"Of course…Cassandra Duncan Support Center…
…that's exactly who we are!"

After consulting with Cassandra's family, Tri-State Rape Crisis and Sexual
Trauma Center hosted a press conference with media and hundreds of
donors in attendance, and announced TSRCSTC would now be named
the CASSANDRA DUNCAN SUPPORT CENTER. Of course, on that

day, and for years to come, each time someone asked, "Who is Cassandra Duncan?" their mission to support donors who cared about hurting women was shared with enthusiasm and passion.

Years later, they dropped "Support," introducing a new statement of mission that read...

...Cassandra Duncan Center supports concerned citizens of the Tri-State, ensuring victims of sexual violence recover and grow strong.

Cassandra Duncan supports concerned citizens of the Tri-State ensuring victims of sexual violence recover and grow strong.

WOW!

Remember where we started. You're our customers...not clients or causes.

INCREASED OVERHEAD IS THE KEY TO NONPROFIT SUCCESS

There are no rules here...we're trying to accomplish something.

~Thomas Edison

Has anyone noticed the new growth industry in the charitable sector? Everywhere you turn, products and services are for sale that deal with the systemic problem of donor attrition. IF YOU BUY "THIS, THAT, or THE OTHER THING," YOU'LL STOP LOSING DONORS!

What? Why are we losing donors in the first place? Supporters increase their giving when cared for with intention. The reason nonprofits face this unnecessary dilemma stems from their lack of understanding that money is more important than mission, donors are more important than clients, causes, or people, AND…

…increased overhead ensures nonprofit success!

Nonprofits with dreams spend money on overhead and salaries! What point on the horizon are you working towards? What dreams make up your vision to tackle problems of global scale?

Here's where strong for-profit enterprise and growth-oriented nonprofits invest their resources:

> **Product** - Strong charities take years to perfect a process that works and changes lives

> **Marketing** - Strong charities spend money to raise the visibility of their cause

> **Sales** - Strong charities organize a veteran team of fundraisers to generate revenue

> **Capital** - Strong charities secure, leverage, and expend capital to solve global problems

> **Salaries** - Strong charities attract top talent by paying top dollar

> **Invention** - Strong charities invest in creativity, research, and risk

I'll have to stop here, take a moment, and confront the push-back I'm sure to get regarding the idea that nonprofits should run more like for-profit business. There is a recent school of thought, advanced by author Jim Collins in his book, *Good to Great and the Social Sectors,* from lines like the one you'll find on page one:

"We must reject the idea—well-intentioned, but dead wrong—that the primary path to greatness in the social sectors is to become 'more like a business.'"

I find this assertion to be a bit sophomoric…

…and on to page twelve of this same book…

"Ironic: Social sector organizations increasingly look to business for leadership models and talent, yet I suspect we will find more true leadership in social sectors than the business sector."

Though I don't doubt the nonprofit sector has something to offer the for-profit sector, the data doesn't support Collin's assertions.

For-profit corporations tackle issues of scale using sound business practice. Nonprofits face the same opportunities around the world and hardly make a dent. As I mentioned earlier in the text, Dan Pallotta reminded us in his Ted Talk, "The way we think about charity is dead wrong," that over the past forty years, 46,136 for-profit businesses grew their revenues past the $50 million dollar mark, while only 144 nonprofit enterprises reached that same level during the same time period.

I've spent my entire adult life simultaneously growing both a for-profit and nonprofit enterprise, and have empirically proven that…

…our sector is saddled with a countless number of irrevocably broken systems that can only be corrected through the application of proven enterprise principles.

Back to the six keys to nonprofit growth—Product, Marketing, Sales, Capital, Salaries, and Invention. How many executive directors do you know that have mastered these six areas of growth? Few, I'll bet, and here's the reason why.

There's this timeless question that American and European donors sling around with impunity.

"How much of my gift is spent on overhead?"

Here are the facts…NONPROFITS DON'T SPEND ENOUGH MONEY ON OVERHEAD, AND SUFFER BECAUSE OF IT.

Nonprofits don't spend enough money on overhead and suffer because of it.

The idea that investing in overhead is unethical or is mismanagement forces nonprofits to forego what they truly need to accomplish their mission. The better question for the strong nonprofit CEO is, *"How do you measure success?"*

Most nonprofit corporations are overseen by the Secretary of State where they are incorporated. There was one particular state whose secretary wanted to clamp down on nonprofits who spent too much of their income on fundraising. So, each Christmas, he placed every nonprofit on an "Angels and Demons List," providing the public guidance regarding their holiday giving. It was pretty simple…if your overhead was high, you're a "demon," if it's low, you're an "angel." He preferred that overhead not exceed 25% of gross revenue; you could still be on the Angels List if you were under 30%, but you really needed to lower your costs.

Here's what happened last year:

Hope Clothing Bank*   **ANGEL**
25% Overhead   75% Cause   2000 Families Served
$370,000 Gross $92,000 Overhead $270,000 Direct

House of Hearts*   **DEMON**
45% Overhead   55% Cause   300 Families Served
$5.5m Gross $2.4m Overhead $3.1m Direct

Basically, if you gave a dollar to House of Hearts, *only 50 cents went to the cause, and the rest to administrative overhead and fundraising.* It gets worse: *House of Hearts took the money that was left over and used it as collateral to secure $10 Million in loans with local banks.*

Here are some more facts. The clothing bank raised $370,000 through an annual banquet, Christmas and Easter mail appeals, and support from local churches. They spent 75% of their gross revenues stocking three strategically located storefronts (donated by the community), providing clothing and furniture to over 2000 families.

House of Hearts spent $2.2 million on major gifts fundraising, awareness events, billboards, television, and direct mail, grossing $5.5 million. They planned to take the remaining $2.8 million, purchase 4 apartment complexes (24 units each) for $740,000 each, providing 90 homeless families a safe place to live. Instead, they took their $2.8 million net profit and secured $10 million dollars in loans, purchasing 13 apartment complexes ($740,000 each, containing 24 units), providing 320 families homes for their hearts.

House of Hearts spent half their money on fundraising, their debt-to-income ratio was over-the-top, and they landed on the state's Demons List. WOULD YOU LIKE TO KNOW WHY?

*names have been changed to protect confidentiality

Because increased overhead is the key nonprofit success! They were aggressive and innovative and provided 320 families a home.

What type of mega-plans is your favorite nonprofit entertaining? Here's a question every philanthropist should ask a nonprofit before investing:

"Can I see a copy of your *Forbes' Top 200 Nonprofits* Strategic Plan?"

You'll get a puzzled look, so clarify by saying, "You know, your plan for strategic growth that lands you on Forbes' Annual List of the Top 200 Nonprofits!"

Let me tell you about two special nonprofit practitioners who left me with a lasting impression.

A few years back, National Development Institute was hosting a Major Gifts Ramp-Up Conference at Columbia International University. Natalie Carlisle, a fellow veteran fundraiser, attended (in part to secure continuing education units [CEUs] to maintain her Certified Fundraising Executive [CFRE] designation). Soon after, we agreed that everyone would benefit if Natalie joined our firm, sharing her vast major gifts experience with the nonprofits we serve. Within a few months, Natalie and I were on stage together, administrating yet another Major Gifts Ramp-Up Conference, this time at the Prime Osborne Center in Jacksonville, FL. It was during this event that we met the team from Food for the Poor (FFTP), who attended to explore expanding their major gifts program. Angel Aloma, FFTP's executive director, was present, and led the charge as their team sorted out major gifts fundraising. Angel explained that Food for the Poor started in Jamaica in 1982 by a "mom and pop" who simply shared some of the food they had with another family in need. Since that time, Food for the Poor grew into North America's largest international relief organization, feeding millions of families every year in 17 Caribbean and Latin American countries. FFTP provides emergency relief assistance, clean water, medicines, educational materials, homes, support for orphans and the aged, skills training, and micro-enterprise development assistance, ensuring others experience a life worth living.

During one of our networking breaks, I approached Angel to introduce myself. Though he was cordial, he was obviously distracted. He excused himself quickly and went to the rear of the conference hall to answer a phone call. He returned a few minutes later and with a broad smile and shared the news, *"We just made Forbe's Top Ten Nonprofits of the Year"*.

He returned a few minutes later with a smile, and shared the good news: *"We just made Forbes' Top Ten Nonprofits of the Year."*

His declaration startled me! I've been in the charitable space my entire adult life and never experienced a moment quite like that one. *How many executive directors do you know who grow their organization in a way that lands them on a Forbes list?*

FFTP went ahead and made a commitment to implement our Major Gifts Ramp-Up Program, retaining Natalie to head up this project. Before long, Angel invited Natalie to join Food for the Poor full-time as their new vice president for Major Gifts.

Natalie called me, and not only shared how Angel had honored her important work, but also revealed the solid salary package he had offered. I won't get into the specifics, but let's just say that earlier this year, *The Chronicle of Philanthropy* announced that Natalie Carlisle was one of the top ten highest paid fundraising professionals in the United States! *Her success is a testimony to her professional abilities and Food for the Poor's aggressive commitment to growth.*

Now that's a nonprofit that has a great dream backed by a sound plan!

So look around—how many organizations do you support that know that money is more important than mission? The bigger the bottom-line, the greater the impact. The more money secured, the more lives are transformed.

RESTRICT YOUR GIVING TO CAPACITY BUILDING

*A farmer's capacity to produce is directly
related to the health of his or her soil.*

~Howard Warren Buffet

In 2013, National Development Institute, in partnership with Clemson University, performed a clinical study, interviewing 470 executive directors who completed a 90 question survey regarding capacity building. This project was overseen by Dr. Kathleen Robinson and supported by National Development Institute staff.

Here were just some of our many findings:

> 90% of nonprofits have a mission statement
> 50% of nonprofits have a vision statement
> 30% of nonprofits have a strategic plan
> *Only 12% of nonprofits have a written fundraising plan*

Nonprofit organizations who believe...

> ...Money is more important than mission
> ...Donors are more important than causes or people
> ...Increased overhead is the key to nonprofit success...

...take the time and money to build organizational capacity.

The term capacity-building has been bandied about our industry for the last two decades, and has taken on a myriad of meanings. The subject matter experts at National Development Institute have spent the last quarter century tackling this issue:

DEFINITION OF <u>CAPACITY BUILDING</u>

> 1: Capacity: the ability to do, experience, or understand something
> 2: Building: the process or business of constructing something

Simply put, capacity building is the method in which a nonprofit secures the resources, structures, skills, and knowledge they require to achieve full potential. *Savvy philanthropists give charities restricted gifts dedicated to capacity building structures that result in long-term financial sustainability!*

Savvy donors give charities restricted gifts dedicated to capacity building structures that result in long-term financial sustainability!

National Development Institute hosts Major Gifts Ramp-Up Conferences all over Asia, Europe, Caribbean, the Middle East, and the U.S. At each of these events (regardless of country or culture) we're confronted with the same short-sighted ideology. It goes something like this. Someone will raise their hand, most likely an executive director, and declare...

> **We want to do this, but we don't have
> the time, money, or staff to fundraise.**

PLEASE FIRE THIS PERSON…TODAY!

I'm not kidding. We have the data. Tragically, most nonprofits are run by weak executive directors, who further disqualify themselves by coming to our events and saying, in front of large groups of people…*we don't have the time, money, or staff to fundraise!*

Here's the root of their self-deception.

I've personally served thousands of organizations around the the world. In all my travels, I've never, not one time, met a nonprofit (regardless of size or budget) that didn't have the time, money, or staff to fundraise.

You see, successful charities stop serving people or causes and instead invest their money, time and staff resources in capacity building.

Successful charities stop serving people or causes and instead invest their money, time, and staff resources in capacity building.

Since I don't have the authority to fire the wonderful and sincere participants who attend our events, I kindly share with them a line from blues composer Tom Delaney:

"Everybody wants to go to heaven, nobody wants to die."

I then ask, "What type of program do you run?" In one instance, an executive director replied, "We provide twenty-four hour residential care to children." I replied, "So you run a children's home."

He replied, "Yes."

I replied, "Ok…well, that's easy…

…STOP TAKING IN KIDS!"

You are a respected philanthropist. I'm imploring you today to invest in capacity building. Start by teaching a nonprofit that you love and support simple fifth grade mathematics. Help them understand how you forecast growth. Share with them the principles you applied when investing resources that worked to expand your enterprise. *Sit down and patiently explain,*

> "Give yourself four years. Year one, downsize program staff and spend these available dollars on capacity building. Year two, begin to receive the financial return on your investment. Year three, use the new monies to hire four times the amount of program staff that you fired. By end of year four, your net increase in children served will exceed all previous records, despite the fact you didn't serve any kids for two years during that same 48 month period of time. You've secured your finances, and will now serve 12,000 children over the next ten years, compared to 3,000 in the previous decade."

RE-IMAGINING PHILANTHROPY THE MOVEMENT begins by making sure nonprofits think differently about MONEY!

Conclusion:

The healthy flow of money is the key. When a nonprofit properly prioritizes revenue generation (oxygen), the charity's approach to MANAGEMENT, MEANS, METHODS, and MODELS are forever transformed.

RIP QUIZ #3

1. Respond to this statement: "Money is more important than mission (or ministry)."

2. Are you comfortable with the statement that follows? "Donors are more important than causes or people."

3. If your answer to the question above is no, write down your reasons. If your answer is yes, write down your reasons.

4. What's the difference between a CEO and an executive director? Please explain.

5. Respond to this statement: "Nonprofit executives need to be paid more money."

6. Have you ever made a gift to a restricted to capacity-building?

7. What nonprofit do you know that should seek to make it onto the Forbes List?

THE MANAGEMENT

God first made idiots (that was for practice) then He made boards.

~Mark Twain

VOLUNTEER BOARDS DON'T WORK AND NEVER WILL

After spending twenty-five years in nonprofit management (having worked with over 500 boards) I've determined, broadly speaking, there are three types of boards...

...mediocre ones, useless ones, and really bad ones.

It's not the fault of the individual volunteer (most of the time), it's simply a flawed business model that never had a chance to succeed.

Here's what your contemporaries have to say:

> *"Effective governance by a board of trustees is a relatively rare and unnatural act. Trustees are often little more than high-powered, well-intentioned people engaged in low-level activities."* ~Thomas Holland

> *"There is one thing all boards have in common...they do not function."* ~Peter Drucker

> *"Ninety-five percent (of boards) are not doing what they are legally, morally, and ethically supposed to do."* ~Harold Geneen

"Board members are usually intelligent and experienced persons as individuals. Yet boards, as groups, are mediocre. Boards tend to be, in fact, incompetent groups of competent individuals." ~John Carver

"Boards have been largely irrelevant throughout most of the twentieth century." ~James Gillies

By and large, the vast majority of volunteer board members do not have the time, experience, or skills necessary to manage a good CEO. *So inevitably, instead of the members managing the CEO, the CEO is tasked with the annoying responsibility of managing the board.* It's a complete waste of time and effort.

By the way, great leaders are not *"managed" in* the first place!

Furthermore, it doesn't matter how big or small the organization may be (e.g. major universities vs. the local animal rescue) boards don't work and never will because…THEY'RE MADE UP OF VOLUNTEERS WHO HAVE A LIMITED KNOWLEDGE OF NONPROFIT ENTERPRISE.

(The reason I referenced major universities came after a review of how Penn State's board of directors handled their recent sex-abuse scandal. This group of accomplished and esteemed trustees collectively demonstrated incompetency one would expect from an ill-equipped local high-school booster club.)

So here's what civil society has decided is the best way to grow a nonprofit enterprise. Let's saddle a CEO with a group of disengaged volunteers, who may or may not regularly gather to share their opinions. *Each board member is equal to the others and gets a full hearing, regardless of their competencies.* This group is all-powerful and is accountable TO NO ONE.

It's unnatural. It's never worked. It never will.

Simply put, THE EMPEROR HAS NO CLOTHES and no one is discussing effective alternatives.

How is it that the oversight of our sector (upon which society relies for safety, health, and provision) could be left to the mediocrity of disengaged volunteers?

But Jimmy, what about those successful nonprofits? Don't they have great boards?

Don't kid yourself! Successful nonprofits are not run by boards; they're run by strong CEOs, in spite of the board. Another way to look at it goes something like this…what would GE, Apple, or Amazon look like today if they had been managed by a disengaged volunteer board of directors?

What would GE, Apple, or Amazon look like today if they had been managed by a disengaged volunteer board of directors?

Let's take a moment and review a traditional organizational chart and standard board member job description. You'll recognize them…they're similar to the ones you'll find in the board orientation manual of most nonprofits. *What follows is fantasy and comes straight from the libraries of our most respected industry experts…and is delusional.*

What follows is fantasy and comes straight from the libraries of our most respected industry experts…*and is delusional.*

DELUSION - Traditional Organizational Chart (15 Plus Members):

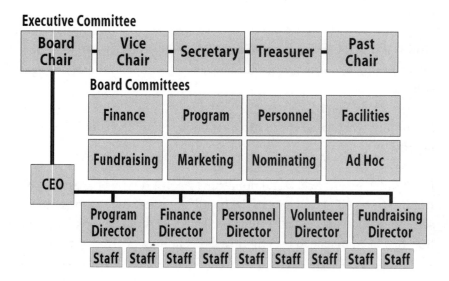

DELUSION - Board Member Purpose: To advise, govern, oversee policy and direction, and assist with the leadership and general promotion so as to support the organization's mission and needs.

DELUSION - Board Member Responsibilities:

- Organizational leadership and advisement
- Expansion of the board of directors, officers, and committees
- Formulation and oversight of policies, procedures, and by-laws
- Financial management, including adoption and oversight of budget
- Oversight of program planning and evaluation
- Personnel evaluation and staff development
- Review of organizational and programmatic reports
- Promotion of the organization
- Fundraising and outreach

DELUSION - Length of term: Three years, which may be renewed up to a maximum of three consecutive terms, pending approval of the board.

DELUSION - Meetings and time commitment: The board of directors meets September through June on the second Monday of the month, 7:00 p.m., Meetings typically last two hours. Committees of the board meet an average of six times per year, pending their respective work agenda.

DELUSION - Expectations of board members:

- Attend meetings on a regular basis, and special events as able.
- Participate on one standing committee, and serve on ad-hoc committees as necessary.
- Be alert to community needs that can be addressed by our mission.
- Help promote mission and program to the community.
- Become familiar with finances, budget, and financial/resource needs.
- Understand the policies and procedures.
- Financially support in a manner commensurate with one's ability.

-END-

OK...WOW! Here's the point. UNREALISTIC EXPECTIONS THAT CAN NEVER BE FULFILLED (and that was the short form!)

I'll spare you from having to review the expanded fifty-page board member's manual containing, amongst other things, board retreats, strategic planning responsibilities and multiple committee assignments. The few times boards are able to fool themselves into thinking that they've fulfilled the responsibilities outlined above only occur when a strong CEO and multiple staff members spend countless hours doing the work for them.

Which is why, in a recent conversation, a CEO shared, **"We work hard to support our trustees...I don't mind doing it...I simply have no idea what it gets me."**

IT GETS WORSE!

Now, take the magnitude of all those written responsibilities, and then pick and choose from the following menu of dysfunctions.

1. Boards formed by people affected by an issue (e.g., parents of kids with cancer)
2. Boards who insist that current clients serve as voting members
3. Boards who have been formed by program participants
4. Boards with members who were invited to join because of social status or popularity
5. Boards who have secured members based on need for diversity
6. Boards made up of members on a crusade
7. Boards comprised of service providers
8. Boards with members who live out of town
9. Boards comprised of pastors
10. Boards comprised of members with emotional disorders
11. Boards whose members don't attend meetings
12. Boards comprised of other nonprofit executives
13. Boards with members who were secured because they're rich
14. Boards with members who are incompetent

IT GETS WORSE!

Now, take all those responsibilities, pick and choose your dysfunctions, and then multiply it by Myers-Briggs sixteen different personality types.

IT GETS WORSE!

...take all the different responsibilities outlined in the job description
...pick and choose from the menu of fifteen dysfunctions
...multiply it by the sixteen different Myers-Briggs personality types
...then add the different sector elements...health, education, human welfare, the arts, environment & religion

Now, gather these individuals in a room once a month, for what too often turns into a two hour group therapy session, facilitated by a clinician (the CEO), whose boss(es) (or patients-in-denial) wouldn't believe for a second that they're the ones with a problem.

I know all boards aren't this way. I ALSO KNOW EVERYONE READING THIS PAGE HAS BEEN IN MEETINGS LIKE THE ONE I DESCRIBED.

This is insane…no, really…this is insane, and must end now. It hasn't ever worked, and never will.

Here's where we're at…this guy walks up to a Coke machine and puts in four quarters. The machine takes his money but nothing comes out. He bangs on the side of the machine, and then carefully drops more coins into the receptacle. Again…nada, nothing comes out, so he bangs and then kicks the machine, but nothing drops. Third time's a charm; he picks through a handful of change and, once again, gets NOTHING…so he bangs, he kicks, he rocks it back and forth and finally notices…

…THE BLASTED MACHINE ISN'T EVEN PLUGGED IN.

Please stop putting money in a machine that ain't got no Coke in it?

By the way, I FIGURED THIS MESS OUT. *Let me tell you about* ***GREAT BOARDSMANSHIP.***

Here's what it's not:

> -Boardsmanship is not Volunteerism
> -Boardsmanship is not Governance
> -Boardsmanship is not Visioning
> -Boardsmanship is not Policy-Making

Boardsmanship is not Governance. Don't kid yourselves. UNPAID BOARD MEMBERS DON'T GOVERN. Actual governance occurs when a person (with a full-time salary) supported by various paid staff (the formation of a government) is empowered to perform the daily tasks of decision-making and oversight. Strong CEOs GOVERN!

Boardsmanship is not Visioning. VISION is the way MISSION is achieved and is never the responsibility of the board because the board isn't being paid to accomplish it. STRONG CEOs ARE TRUSTED TO CREATE VISION. (I agree that board members hold their compensated leader accountable to achieve MISSION.) Here's what you do. Hire a strong CEO who has a history of designing VISION that accomplishes MISSION in ways you never dreamed possible. Believe me, strong CEOs are already doing it their way even if they feel the need to label their activities as "BOARD VISION."

Boardsmanship is not Policy-Making. Hire a CEO whose depth of experience and formal education has already equipped them as a management expert. The right CEO has been properly trained to oversee the creation of policies that work. Board Members never write policy anyway. Someone else does the heavy-lifting and they rubber stamp it.

Boardsmanship is not Volunteerism: Eliminate the special events committee. Eliminate the fundraising committee. Eliminate the public relations committee. Eliminate the strategic planning committee. (Here's a good rule of thumb - remove everything from your by-laws that's not related to IRS compliance.) Re-assemble these groups as volunteers (non-board members) who serve you directly. For example, a group of social workers is assembled to serve the program director, or a campaign cabinet comprised of community volunteers is built to advance fundraising. You now have individuals in their sweet spots, who are no longer saddled with arcane tasks.

Boardsmanship is not Management: Board members have no authority over the day-to-day operations of a nonprofit UNLESS there's a written directive recorded in board meeting minutes with a motion, second and full vote. Members cannot unilaterally exercise power. Nor can committees. Conversely, board members actually need to receive permission from the CEO if they intend to act on behalf of the nonprofit in a manner that could affect daily operations.

OK, OK...what is ***GREAT BOARDSMANSHIP?***

(everything you need on one page - please copy and send to everyone)

Great boards provide two things.

...ADVICE & ACCOUNTABILITY

The STRONG CEO is named chair of the nominations committee and fills these SIX POSITIONS (yes, you only need six [plus]):

1. Business Expert	(Chair)	Entrepreneur
2. Program Expert	(Secretary)	Specific
3. Finance Expert	(Treasurer)	Accountant
4. Legal Expert	(Member)	Lawyer
5. Communications Expert	(Member)	PR/Marketer
6. Nonprofit Expert	(Member)	Consultant
7. Plus (as needed)	(Member)	Consultant

THAT'S IT! *(add other experts as needed eg. personnel, etc.)* However, don't forget, working group theory states that any "working group" with **more than seven** people *is no longer a group that works!*

Here are their ten <u>ADVICE & ACCOUNTABILITY</u> functions:

1. Comply with IRS Regulations
2. Hire strong Chief Executive Officer
3. Approve Meeting Agenda
4. Approve and Amend By-Laws
5. Choose and Review Independent <u>Financial</u> Audit (annual)
6. Choose and Review Independent <u>Program</u> Audit (annual)
7. Evaluate strong Chief Executive Officer
8. Attend Three Meetings per Year with Recorded Minutes
9. Support the CEOs Vision (not the boards vision)
10. Provide CEO their expert advice

MAKE YOUR CEO THE CHAIRMAN OF THE BOARD
(it's OK...she already is)

CEO Responsibilities:

1. CEO (**may or may not**) be named Chairman of the Board
2. CEO nominates board members
3. CEO has one vote
4. CEO writes meeting agenda
5. Board members approve meeting agenda
6. CEO is recused from vote regarding hiring of auditors

Better Board Organizational Chart (6 members)

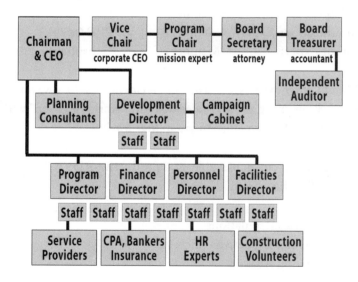

What would happen if every nonprofit CEO had the privilege and the power to build his or her own board of directors? What would happen if they had boards they could call their own?

First, re-write the by-laws, making the CEO chairman of the board. By the way, this is the way it's already working anyway. Don't kid yourself;

successful nonprofits with volunteer boards ARE ALREADY BEING RUN BY THE CEO! The smart CEO already gets the votes he/she needs from disengaged volunteer board members before the meeting. There is an ongoing debate among board governance experts, who not only agree that CEOs should be voting members of the board, *but should also be installed as chair of the organization they're responsible to lead.*

Tragically, the nonprofit sector has made it clear that the CEO does not fill the role of board chair, and even consider this humorous maxim a "best practice." *We've deceived ourselves into believing that having a volunteer in this position ensures a kind of objectivity and fiduciary well-being for the nonprofit.* We also believe that too much power would be given to the CEO, and members wouldn't be able to fulfil their fiduciary responsibilities, when the exact opposite is true. The strong CEO is the one person who constantly supports the board, saving them from embarrassment and their own irresponsibility.

Second, allow the CEO to build his own board team by hiring six leaders from the community and paying them a generous honorarium *per meeting* for their excellent board craft. I've seen this work and work well. By the way, you will never have a member miss a meeting ever again!

Look at Steve Jobs. He made six people he trusted directors of his board. The board hired a third party financial auditor to represent the company's finances to these members. Together, they built a multi-million dollar empire. Years later, his friends fired him as CEO. Years after that, these same friends brought him back. In his first meeting, he shared, "YOU WERE RIGHT...I NEEDED TO BE FIRED...LET'S GET TO WORK!"

They went on to build a multi-BILLION dollar empire.

Let's let nonprofit CEOs build their own leadership team. The charitable sector doesn't have a prayer otherwise.

Here's what Mike Burns, governance expert recently wrote: "Why should board members be concerned (about installing their CEO as board chair)? While many folks are afraid of flying, they forget that the pilot has as much of an incentive to bring the passengers to their destination as they do to get there. I propose that boards that worry about CEOs serving as board chairs should remember that CEOs want great outcomes as much as board members do."

SUCCESSFUL BOARDS REALLY AREN'T BOARDS

I keep purporting that this type of nonprofit governance is already happening in some sort of "stealth mode" within the sector.

Take a look at a well-run local United Way.

I've spent my entire career around United Way CEOs. Presently, National Development Institute has three United Way execs serving on our faculty. When you get two of them together, by themselves, behind closed doors, all they do is quiz each other about their current board chairs.

Here's their winning formula:

STRONG CEO + CHAIRPERSON
YOU'RE LOOKIN' AT THE ENTIRE BOARD

The following organizational chart and committee descriptions can be found in standard United Way local chapter board manuals. **I've also included their description matrix,** *to demonstrate that very few United Way Board Member Job Responsibilities actually have anything to do with board governance.*

What you are about to see is not a board of directors, but rather a well-heeled expert volunteer coordinator (the CEO) with the financial resources he or she needs to provide local community leaders a superior

volunteer experience. THE SECRET TO THEIR SUCCESS LIES IN
THEIR ABILITY TO STAFF EACH "BOARD COMMITTEE" with one
or more full time employees.

United Way Organizational Chart (25 Members)

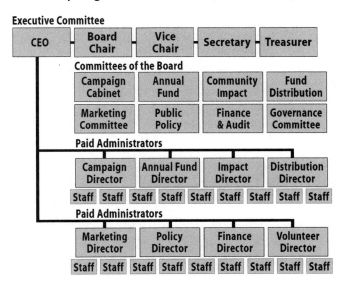

Please flip to the back of the book and take a quick peek at the United
Way Committee Descriptions in Appendix B. What you'll discover there
is not a governing board, but rather a group of volunteers whose success
is directly related to the number of staff members supporting them in
their good work.

It works for the United Way (UW), and I applaud them. However, at the
end of the day, this is mostly possible because the United Way provides
little or no direct services to the community. Your local UW, unlike many
nonprofits, has the money to invest in their volunteer structures. Another
way of looking at it is…YES, the UW DOES provide direct services.

*THEY PROVIDE DIRECT SERVICES TO THE VOLUNTEERS WHO
SERVE ON THEIR COMMITTEES AND BOARD OF DIRECTORS.*

STRONG CEOs ARE THE KEY TO BUILDING CAPACITY
(NOT STRONG BOARDS)

After years of applying countless board theories to real world nonprofits, one could suppose that John Carver came close with his model, but ultimately failed nonprofit enterprise. Even Carver saddled the strong CEO with responsibilities to volunteers who never should have been in authority in the first place. Unfortunately, the data indicates that boards who embraced the Carver Model are as useless today as they were thirty years ago.

Allow me to cite, yet again, our collaboration with Clemson University.

NDI, in partnership with Clemson, performed a study using a clinical sample of 470 executive directors who participated in a 90 question survey regarding capacity building. *The focus of the study was to investigate the relationship between the efficacy of capacity building and the intentions of the organization's leadership to embark upon capacity building. This was a necessary behavioral study, in that previous works failed to show any empirical data regarding the relationship between a nonprofit's ABILITY TO BUILD CAPACITY and the actual return on the investment made in time, human resource, and monies spent on capacity building.*

Here's what we discovered regarding a nonprofit's ability to build capacity:

1. Lack of Return-On-Investment

The majority of organizational development/capacity-building investments made by foundations, corporations, or individuals have failed to produce lasting changes in the operations/infrastructure of nonprofits that attempted to build capacity.

2. Organizations that did build capacity

Organizations that <u>were</u> successful at demonstrating a measurable return-on-investment in capacity building were *led by extraordinary executives (CEOs/Presidents/Executive Directors)*. These executives possessed specific attitudes, beliefs, and skills sets. They also took personal responsibility for project implementation and outcomes.

3. What Successful CEOs Accomplished

> a. They built more capacity over a five year period than those nonprofits who indicated they stagnated or declined during the same time period.
>
> b. They grew budget, programs & donors, despite the recession.
>
> c. They grew their nonprofits regardless of the size or involvement of their board.
>
> d. They externalized the mission of their organization for the purpose of fundraising.
>
> e. They developed board members who evaluated the chief executive and promoted the goals and values of the CEO.

The greatest contribution we can make to the nonprofit sector is to do whatever it takes to attract, pay and empower great CEOs.

The greatest contribution we can make to the nonprofit sector is to do whatever it takes to attract, pay and empower CEOs.

REAL BOARDS DON'T FUNDRAISE

To get him to agree, I put a gun to his head.
To get him to not change his mind, I blew out his brains.

~Jarod Kintz

Here's what you do…

Find fifteen busy community leaders…ask them do 120 hours of free work per year…then ask them to PAY YOU to do the free work… after they have paid, explain that the work you need them to do is something they have never done, are not good at, and will make them uncomfortable!

It defies reasoning, does it not? Yet, fundraising professionals around the world peddle this silliness, despite the fact that it doesn't work. Here's an article I read this week from a leading expert on board development.

> *Should board members fundraise? Why not? Seriously, I don't get this one at all. If your governing body is free to make strategic and programmatic decisions without understanding, first hand, the financial implications of those decisions, you are setting your nonprofit up for failure…Let's stop apologizing for having to make money in the nonprofit sector and start requiring every single board member get actively involved in the process.*

I have a sense that the author may have forgotten that:

-Board service is not a board member's job
-Board members join boards to network and enjoy themselves
-Board members are not motivated by guilt
-Board members respond to accountability differently than staff
-Board members may not have the skills to do face-to-face "asking"
-Board members may not want to do face-to-face fundraising

Furthermore, well-run boards understand that fundraising IS NOT an ADVICE & ACCOUNTABILITY function and that mandating it can demoralize members who are already performing a very important service.

BUT WAIT, JIMMY…that's why it is so important to provide regular board training.

Each year, hundreds of millions of dollars leave the charitable sector and end up in the bank accounts of publishers and consultants **_who are peddling swill_** (by the way, I am both a publisher and consultant who in the past has been a swill peddler).

Training is key to growing an enterprise. In days gone by, cross-trainers would test an employee in four separate disciplines. If, out of the four, he or she performed as low as 35% in one area, they'd go ahead and invest training dollars to improve performance in that particular discipline. Someone finally looked at the data, and discovered that after proper training and re-testing, the employee's performance moved from 35% up to a whopping 43%—which subsequently disqualified them from working in that area, and also indicated that training them had little or no effect.

Here's my point; place gifted volunteers in positions that they love. Invite them to perform tasks they enjoy and already do well.

Place gifted volunteers in positions that they love. Invite them to perform tasks they enjoy and already do well.

Here is what Dr. John Curtis (a dear friend and NDI's organizational development expert) said to me years ago…

"Jimmy…never try to teach a pig to sing;
it wastes your time and it annoys the pig."

Here's the good news. Fundraising may not be the board's responsibility, but is still a key volunteer function that's a whole lot easier to do if you ***build a non-governing campaign cabinet comprised of veteran fundraisers who are really good at asking for money!***

Let me tell you about Charlotte Berry.

I've worked on various projects with Charlotte for over a decade, and am one of many witnesses to her extraordinary example of what it means to be a volunteer fundraiser. Charlotte is also one of National Development Institute's greatest champions. I'm personally grateful for our friendship.

Charlotte began collecting dimes from classmates for her school's Junior Red Cross chapter at age twelve. Today, at age eighty-four, she continues in that same tradition as a national spokesperson for the value of philanthropy, and volunteerism. Over the years, she's generated millions of dollars for various community causes through her own personal gifts ***as well as through the solicitation of public and private funds from others***. She's served on bank boards, college boards, led cultural arts projects, and co-founded various groups, including Women in Philanthropy. Her national service to both the American Red Cross and the United Way of America further demonstrate her unwavering commitment to grow the charitable sector.

Charlotte will testify that one of her most important responsibilities is to involve people in philanthropy for the first time. She enjoys helping others find the right fit for what they have to offer e.g. volunteer work, a board position, or a financial gift they hadn't previously considered. She strongly believes that everyone should experience what it feels like to give back, and is fond of saying, *"Do something every day to feel good."*

Simply put, in our town, if you're about to launch a fundraising campaign you want Charlotte to be at the helm.

Here's what I'm trying to get at:

First, most volunteer board members are not a...

...*"CHARLOTTE BERRY!"*

Second, every successful fundraising campaign needs a...

...*"CHARLOTTE BERRY!"*

Any nonprofit that's about to tackle a multi-million dollar fundraising campaign must patiently wait for their champion to emerge. Charlotte is a well-heeled philanthropist who built friendships with prominent families and leaders in every community she's called home. Her capacity to SECURE & ORGANIZE a team of fellow-volunteers who both "give" and "ask" is the difference between fundraising success and failure.

Here are your options:

#1 Demoralize board members by insisting they do something they can't or won't do.

...or instead...

#2 Find a veteran fundraiser who will inspire the right people to join and fundraise for your campaign.

All I'm trying to say is let board members be board members! Let fundraisers be fundraisers! Don't require board members to be something they're not! Give every volunteer a job that they love! Live and let live!

Let board members be board members! Let fundraisers be fundraisers! Don't require board members to be something they're not!

Conclusion:

RE-IMAGINING PHILANTHROPY...MOVEMENT is best served when both MONEY and MANAGEMENT are viewed through the lens of enterprise. *Here's another way to look at it:*

Have you been successful in enterprise? Have you ever served on a board?

Would the nonprofit board you served on have been helpful, harmful, or no help at all in making your enterprise successful? What would have happened if your fellow volunteer board members were put in charge of running your business? Hmmm? Then why do it to nonprofit CEOs?

What would have happened if your fellow board members were put in charge of running your business? Hmmm? Then why do it to nonprofit CEOs?

I'm just asking!

RIP QUIZ #4

1. Have you ever served on a nonprofit board of directors?

2. Would you allow the board of directors with whom you've served oversee your own personal enterprise?

3. If you answered yes to the question above, please share the reasons why. If you answered no, please share the reasons why.

4. Respond to this statement: "Nonprofits thrive when led by a strong CEO, regardless of their board of directors."

5. Respond to this statement: "Make your executive director the chairman of your board."

6. After reading this chapter, do you understand the difference between governing and volunteering? Does the board you serve on lean towards governance only, or more towards volunteering?

7. Name five things you would change about boards of directors and the way they traditionally operate.

8. Have you served on a board of directors that required you to fundraise? If you answered yes, please describe your fundraising experience.

THE MEANS

*Trust is the glue of life…it's the
foundational principle that holds all relationships.*

~Stephen Covey

TRUE FUNDRAISING…
…FIND A NEED AND MEET IT…
…MAKE A PROMISE AND KEEP IT!

My goal for this section is to take you behind the scenes and provide you some select insights about how you (the donor) operate. I'd also like to help you sort out what works for you when you give, guide, and support charities.

The biggest obstacle we face in renovating civil society will not be boards, nonprofits, or consultants. The problem we'll first have to tackle will be the misconceptions held by *you!*

Why? Because this idea that *donors are a nonprofit's primary customer* will give YOU pause.

Our puritanical roots have warped our perspectives on giving. Tragically, millennial old distortions of Judeo-Christian ethics have falsely led people to believe that if there is some sort of personal inurement attached to gift-giving, the value of the act is neutralized and without merit.

Charity is not penance…charity is not a tax…charity is not a toll. The word "charity" comes from the Greek word *charis* and means…REJOICE, REJOICE, REJOICE!!!

Charities who understand *true fundraising* will bring out the **best** in you…will bring out the **most** in you…will bring out your **finest gift** ever and, in turn, provide millions in need a life worth living. Nonprofits who prioritize trust building will provide you an experience so graceful, that you 'll say in your heart, "I can't wait to do that again, again…and again!"

Nonprofits who prioritize trust building provide you an experience so graceful, that you'll say in your heart, "I can't wait to do that again…and again…and again!"

These experiences are rooted in a TRUST RELATIONSHIP between both you and the charity. ORGANIZATIONAL TRUST is built on a foundation that ensures your long-term experience is rich, sound, and based on a series of transactions that include:

BUILDING TRUST THROUGH MULTIPLE TRANSACTIONS

1. Values…

…you believe in their mission, *they believe in your mission*

2. Solutions…

…you agree with their approach, *they agree with yours*

3. Personality…

…you like them, they engage you, *they like you, you engage them*)

4. Opportunity...

...you're inspired by their project, *they're inspired by your investment*

5. Abilities...

...you're impressed with their skills, *they're impressed with yours*

6. Orientation...

...you know what makes them tick, *they know what makes you tick*

7. Finances...

...you're confident in their stewardship, *they are confident in yours*

8. Reciprocity...

...you give, *they give,* you become their focus, *they become yours*)

The list above is not glib, nor is it just rhetoric. Allow me to share with you the story of San Antonio Miracle Homes* and how their team relies on these eight transactions to provide donors a superior giving experience.

The next three pages contain sample language that can be used to help a nonprofit get out of themselves and instead reach out to you (the donor.) These narratives demonstrate "donor-centered" communications.

*names and locations in this overview have been changed to protect confidentiality

The next three pages contain sample language that can be used to help a nonprofit get out of themselves and instead center on you, the donor.

SAN ANTONIO MIRACLE HOMES – BUILDING DONOR TRUST

Let's take a peek and see how San Antonio Miracle Homes builds organizational trust. I'll start by sharing a few of the important narratives they provide their friends and supporters. The paragraphs that follow demonstrate how donors are the key to their program.

You see, San Antonio Miracle Homes' Board of Directors and administrators believe that YOU, THE DONOR are their primary customer. Here's their statement of mission:

San Antonio Miracle Homes serves donors and volunteers tasked with eradicating homelessness among San Antonio's senior women, single moms, and their children.

#1 TRANSACTION TYPE...*VALUES*

For some San Antonians, life's losses, low income, disability, or even personal missteps make homeless a family member we call our own. San Antonio Miracle Homes provides San Antonio's concerned community leaders the organizational resources they require to provide our seniors, women, moms, and children the love, support, shelter, and care that makes life worth living.

#2 TRANSACTION TYPE...*SOLUTION*

Community leaders use their finances and networks to provide senior women facing homelessness with permanent housing, who are then paired with single mothers and children living in transition.

Community leaders use their finances and networks to provide senior women facing homelessness with permanent housing, who are then paired with single mothers and children living in transition.

Here's how it works! Donors and volunteers (who make their homes in San Antonio) believe that older citizens find a new calling when matched with young, single moms working towards self-sufficiency. Seniors are provided housing, transportation, medical services, grocery shopping, church services, community activities, and more. Single moms and their children receive support, love and childcare from their elders, job assistance, high-school completion, and the counseling they need to begin building lives for their new families.

#3 TRANSACTION TYPE...*PERSONALITY*

Candice Armstrong, founder and San Antonio native, spends her life in service to our community. During her years as an accomplished business professional, Candice built meaningful friendships with key leaders, local businesses, and corporations who would financially underwrite her dream to serve seniors, moms, and children. One night, Candice (who was once herself a teenage mother) received a vision of grandmotherly women rocking infants, and sitting at their feet were young mothers.

The elder women were sharing their wisdom with teen moms and, in turn, the young were caring for the old. That night, San Antonio Miracle Homes was born.

#4 TRANSACTION TYPE...*ABILITIES*

For nearly two-decades, San Antonio Miracle Homes has worked with donors, volunteers, and community leaders to create programs, policies, and procedures that ensure seniors, moms, and children receive the support they require to live a life worth living.

Here are just a few of the services SAMH provides San Antonians:

- 1 Saint Anthony Leadership Society Awards Gala
- 1 Celebrate San Antonio Volunteer Press Conference
- 1 San Antonio Community Research Council Summit
- 6 Bridge Campaign Cabinet Forums
- 140 Private Meetings with San Antonio Donors and Volunteers
- 1,300 Financial Gifts Facilitated for Seniors, Young Mothers, and Children
- 10,600 Safe Bed Nights
- 7,300 Diapers and Wipes
- 360 Counseling Sessions
- 6,000 Case Management Hours
- 1,000 Bags of Groceries
- 1,200 Household Goods and Furniture
- 3,700 Articles of Clothing
- 1,200 Pairs of Shoes
- 5,100 Daycare Drop-Offs/Pick Ups
- 200 Life Skills Classes

#5 TRANSACTION TYPE...*ORIENTATION*

San Antonio Miracle Homes prioritizes relationships with community leaders, advocates, donors, and volunteers who care about San Antonio's seniors, young moms, and children. SAMH's Saint Anthony Leadership Society (SALS) engages individuals, foundations, and corporations, ensuring their goals for San Antonio are realized. SALS is the heart and soul of SAMH and is based on the creation of individual plans of care for each SALS member, ensuring their year-long annual experience is both meaningful and rich. Simply put, our hearts are turned towards community leaders who have made citizens in need their priority.

#6 TRANSACTION TYPE...*RECIPROCITY*

The success of San Antonio Miracle Homes is rooted in our mission to serve San Antonio's long-standing donors, volunteers, and advocates in a way that works for them. Trust is built by establishing formal partnerships with each donor based on transparency and information sharing. This ensures that everyone has a superior gift-giving experience. SAMH supporters personally see their investment of time and money transform San Antonio. In the end, when new relationships are formed between community leaders and the women and children of SAMH, no one's quite sure who is the greater benefactor, as each person loves and is loved in return.

#7 TRANSACTION TYPE...*FINANCES*

San Antonio Miracle Homes is where San Antonio's donors go to invest. Jack Salinger, SAMH Board Treasurer, Chair of the Finance Committee, and President of the Saint Anthony Leadership Society, announced at last month's SALS Press Conference that $480,000 was invested by SALS members who made San Antonio's seniors, women, and children their personal financial priority. In turn, the SAMH Board and Saint Anthony

Leadership Society re-invested these funds back into our community, providing San Antonio over $1.4 million in transformative services that make life worth living for all of our citizens.

#8 TRANSACTION TYPE...*OPPORTUNITY*

The opportunity before us is a simple one...a great dream backed by· a sound plan. SAMH donors and volunteers have determined that homelessness among senior women and single moms can be eradicated in San Antonio if an additional 280 annual residential placements could be provided to families in need.

SAMH donors have determined that homelessness among senior women and single moms can be eradicated if an additional 280 annual placements are provided to families in need.

Friends and supporters of San Antonio Miracle Homes have committed to raising $4.2 Million over the next 18 months to expand SAMH's existing residential program. This plan includes:

- Building a 42,000 square foot facility, including two residential housing complexes and administrative offices.
- Hiring two additional case managers, a chef and culinary educator, two resident assistants, full-time bookkeeper, volunteer coordinator, and a groundskeeper.
- Expanding our food pantry, diaper bank, and transportation program, including the purchases of two shuttle buses.

OK...HOW DID THAT FEEL?

Whew!!! Does that feel right? Does making trust-building a priority make sense? Understanding that donors are a nonprofit's primary customer ultimately ensures more lives are touched and civil society is made whole. Great nonprofits understand that you (donors) are precious and, when meaningfully engaged, will perform magnanimous acts of generosity that change everything!

All eight of the Trust Transactions listed are imperative. I'd like to share three quick stories that expand on Values, Orientation, and Personality. Proper attention to these three transactions will supercharge your relationship with the charities you already love and support.

Let's start by turning things upside down!

You see…IT'S NOT ABOUT THEIR MISSION…*IT'S ABOUT YOURS*

TRUST TRANSACTION…VALUES
THEY BELIEVE IN YOUR PERSONAL MISSION

Over the course of my career, I have had the opportunity to build "trust relationships" with some of our nation's most iconic families—families who, by anyone's standards, would be considered veteran volunteers and professional givers.

Let me tell you about Louise Slater. She is heir to a steel company fortune, and has served for years as the company's chairperson. Louise is a founding member of Women in Philanthropy, a lifelong United Methodist, and has a strong personality combined with a very generous heart. I'm fond of saying Louise collects broken-things. She gravitates to people and needs that are most unattractive. She grew up in the Deep South, in a wealthy home with loving parents who, like all families, had their share of ups and downs. One factor that significantly impacted her formative years was being raised by an African-American nanny.

Louise was an early champion of National Development Institute (NDI), and on more than one occasion moderated our training events. She always sat in on the sessions, taking notes to be referenced during later conversations.

There was one particular topic that piqued her interest.

You see, we start every NDI event establishing a fundraising philosophy by comparing three separate approaches. We propose that only one really works, and that the other two will kill a nonprofit's program. Here are all three:

#1 Technique Driven Philosophy is based on events, galas, tournaments, direct mail, newsletters, phone campaigns, etc. Techniques can be used, but a *philosophy of development* can't be driven by technique. This type of fundraising isn't sustainable because it's a numbers game, and only works by burning through thousands of prospects.

#2 Institution Driven Philosophy says, "We're making a difference... We're a good steward of donor finances...This organization is a safe place to invest...Blah, Blah, Blah." Here's the problem: it's all about self, self, self. This approach is tiresome, and it is what every other organization is saying, and hasn't worked for fifty years.

THE CORRECT APPROACH
...a donor-driven philosophy of development

#3 Donor Driven Philosophy is "How can we help YOU (the donor) accomplish the personal goals to which you've been called? How do we partner, walk side-by-side, co-labor with, invest in, and ensure that your objectives are considered? You have specific desires...it's the nonprofit's responsibility to understand what they are and make them come true. What are your interests? What constructs in your life cross with the constructs emerging from the organization?" It's at this nexus that "relationship" emerges…and that development occurs.

Let's continue with our story about Louise.

Louise invited me to attend a private event for the Hospital Foundation's upcoming capital campaign. It was an evening cocktail reception with local television personalities and key donors from the community. The president of the foundation introduced a well-crafted case for support, overviewing their intent to build a massive wing to house a new children's hospital.

Six weeks later, Louise called the office and began describing for me the afternoon she wasted touring the hospital with the foundation president. They spent about two hours together, after which the president proposed that she make a six figure gift, accompanied by a significant naming opportunity.

The request was made and Louise responded with,

"We're not going to be involved in this project."

The president than made the mistake of doubling down and asked, "Louise, is that a 'no' or a 'hell no?'"

Louise was not given to coarse language, but in this case replied, "That would be a 'hell no.'"

He said, "I don't understand." She repeated,

"Our family is not going to be involved in this project!"

He said, "Okay," and then uncomfortably escorted her to the parking lot.

She further explained her dismay, and said, "Jimmy, all he did was drone on about his project. He never asked me about our family's goals...you know...that donor-driven philosophy of development we always talk about at our training events!"

Here's the lesson:

Louise was actually a good prospect for the Hospital Foundation for more than one reason. First, her family stewarded a significant amount of wealth, but more importantly...

...Louise lived at that hospital!

Let me explain. Louise spends her time, emotions, and money on kids *WHO ARE POOR*. She provides a means of escape to children, teens, and young adults swallowed up in poverty. She gave big gifts to the Children's Museum, founded Friends of Juvenile Justice, and owns the Price Group (a firm that supports families with troubled sons and daughters who need very sophisticated social work solutions). Her favorite hobby involves taking young teen moms (several at a time) out of the projects, personally mentoring them, and then paying for their college education.

Furthermore, inner city kids do not receive medical care from specialists or doctors in town. Any time there's a problem, they end up in the emergency room, and dear Louise would spend many nights tending to young girls in the Hospital Foundation's ER.

So here's Louise...an accomplished, highly-respected community leader, who lives on the frontline of the war on poverty. She depends on the hospital (the ER) to serve the children she loves. The opportunities to meaningfully involve her in the hospital's mission were countless. What would have happened if the foundation president sought her perspectives regarding real issues that were important to her, the children she served, and the hospital?

I'm just saying...*there was a way.*

Here's what happened next...

...the hospital foundation president *CALLED ME!*

He told me what happened, didn't let me get a word in edgewise, and then repeated over and over, "I don't understand...I just don't understand."

His confusion was easily explained. He hadn't embraced Louise's personal mission. In truth, he had no idea what it was!

He finally asked, "Jimmy, do you know what went wrong?"

He and I were operating in entirely separate universes. I knew it would've been inappropriate to schoolmaster him, so I just mumbled,

"No...hell no."

For me, the greater lesson to be learned was not about the president's missteps, but rather enjoying Louise's journey as she RE-IMAGINED HER OWN PHILANTHROPY. Her encounter with the Hospital Foundation demonstrates that there's room for education and personal growth among donors. She took the time to re-imagine her own philanthropy. She honed her craft and now gives in a way that provides everyone involved a rich and meaningful experience.

Louise re-imagined her own philanthropy by focusing her giving, without apology, on causes that achieved her personal goals.

Our many discussions about a donor-driven approach to development were important to Louise. These ideas resonated with her, and from that point forward, she set boundaries with nonprofits, and focused her philanthropy, without apology, on causes that advanced her goals for our community.

TRUST TRANSACTION…ORIENTATION
THEY KNOW WHAT MAKES YOU TICK

Comprehending your motivations, desires, needs, and goals is the very heart of their "ask." The fundraising practitioners you work with must have a "zen-like" command of the interchangeable elements of your pathos. Like a clock with all its gears, springs, and wheels perfectly balanced to generate observable motion, the fundraising practitioner must know what makes you tick.

Don't forget our definition of being donor-driven: *how can a nonprofit help you accomplish the goals to which you have been called?* How will they partner, walk side-by-side, co-labor with, invest in, and ensure you become part of their family in a manner that considers your needs? You have dreams…it's the nonprofit's responsibility to understand what they are and make them come true. What are your interests? What constructs do you possess that cross with theirs? It's at this nexus that relationships grow…that development occurs.

Expert fundraising practitioners understand the unique type, cause, requirements, and communication preferences that make up your pathos. Effective development officers watch and listen for clues that reveal your intent, and design a path that leads you to a meaningful decision. These clues are used to create individual plans of care, designed to meet your needs, rather than relying on a one-size-fits-all approach.

> These clues are used to create plans of care, *designed to meet your needs*, rather than relying on a one-size-fits-all approach.

Here is the process with which a good development officer seeks to understand what makes you tick. Let's take a moment to review what I call the Major Donor Motivation Matrix.

Donor Motivation Matrix vs. Reasons Donors Give
(LaRose)   *(Panas)*

In the early eighties, Jerry Panas wrote a book called *Mega Gifts*, and included a section named "The Top Twenty One Reasons Donors Give." This resource has been relied upon for nearly three decades, and played an important role in helping practitioners understand what motivates donors. Here are the top twenty-one reasons why you give:

1. You believe in the mission of the institution.
2. You have an interest in a specific program or project.
3. You are provided a meaningful memorial opportunity.
4. You respect the institution locally.
5. You serve on the board or a major committee.
6. You are actually involved in the campaign program.
7. You have been heavily influenced by your peer solicitor.
8. You have a history of being involved in the institution.
9. You have a high regard for the volunteers of the institution.
10. You are faced with upcoming tax considerations.
11. You are taken by the uniqueness of the project or the institution.
12. You enjoy recognition of your gift.
13. You had a need and were served by the institution in the past.

14. You respect their circle of influence —state, nation, region.
15. You give out of a sense of community responsibility or civic pride.
16. You give to challenge or encourage other gifts.
17. You have a high regard for staff leadership.
18. You give a gift to match a gift or gifts made by others.
19. You have a religious/spiritual affiliation with the institution.
20. You believe that the institution is fiscally sound.
21. You were appealed to by the drama of the campaign material.

I have studied Panas' work for twenty-five years. I looked forward to the revised version of *Mega Gifts,* which promised an updated list. Here's the problem: even the newer edition is incomplete and lacks relevance in a twenty-first century fundraising economy. First, his list is anecdotal and does not rely on an empirical survey. Second, more than one "reason" is the same as another (see 5 and 8 or 4 and 9). Finally, the list is incomplete. Number 15 opens up another entire list of unmentioned reasons, by starting a discussion about communitarians, and then failing to list other donor types, such as the dynast, socialite, etc.

I can't over emphasize how important it is that the fundraising pracitioner have a "zen-like" command of the interchangeable elements of your pathos (ideas & emotions)

Or, to put it another way…***a good fundraiser knows what makes you tick!*** The best practitioners truly know why you give, how you give, and to what you give, by distilling your cause type, management requirements, personality, and communication preferences. Let's now take a look at the Major Gifts Ramp-Up Motiviation Matrix, based on statistical surveys peformed by National Development Insititute and other industry leaders.

MAJOR GIFTS RAMP-UP MOTIVATION MATRIX (redux)

TYPE	CAUSE	REQUIREMENTS	PERSONALITY	COMMUNICA
• Communitarian	• Religion	• Shared Values/Mission	• Extraversion	• One-On-One
• Devout	• Education	• Financially Stable	• Introversion	• Phone/Mobile
• Investors	• Human Welfare	• Interest in Project	• Sensing	• Email/Online
• Socialite	• Healthcare	• Staff Leadership	• Intuition	• Social Media
• Repayer	• Public Benefit	• Volunteer Leadership	• Thinking	• Onsite/Tour
• Altruist	• Arts/Culture	• Respected Locally	• Feeling	• Direct Mail
• Dynast	• International	• Respected Nationally	• Judging	• Special Events
	• Environment	• Influence of Solicitor	• Perceiving	• Video/Stream
(Seven Faces of Philanthropy)	• Animals	• Memorial Opportunity		• Collateral Do
		• Gift Recognition	*(Myers-Briggs)*	
		• Challenge Gift		
		• Campaign Cabinet		
		• Board/Committee Service		

MAJOR GIFTS RAMP-UP MOTIVATION MATRIX (expanded)

WHAT TYPE ARE YOU?   (Seven Faces of Philanthropy)

• Communitarian	(26%)	"Doing Good Makes Good Sense"
• Devout	(21%)	"Doing Good is God's Will"
• Investors	(15%)	"Doing Good is Good Business"
• Socialite	(11%)	"Doing Good is Fun"
• Repayer	(10%)	"Doing Good in Return"
• Altruist	(9%)	"Doing Good Feels Right"
• Dynast	(8%)	"Doing Good is a Family Tradition"

WHAT CAUSES DO YOU CARE ABOUT?

• Religion	(31%)	• Arts/Culture	(5%)
• Education	(16%)	• International	(4%)
• Human Welfare	(12%)	• Environment	(3%)
• Healthcare	(10%)	• Animals	(1%)
• Public Benefit	(7%)		

MAJOR GIFTS RAMP-UP MOTIVATION MATRIX (cont.)

WHAT DO YOU REQUIRE FROM A NONPROFIT?

- Shared Values/Mission
- Financially Stable
- Interest in Project
- Staff Leadership
- Volunteer Leadership
- Respected Locally
- Respected Nationally
- Influence of Solicitor
- Memorial Opportunity
- Gift Recognition
- Challenge/Leadership Gift
- Campaign Cabinet
- Board/Committee Service

WHAT PERSONALITY ARE YOU?

• Extraversion	(E)	• Thinking	(T)
• Introversion	(I)	• Feeling	(F)
• Sensing	(S)	• Judging	(J)
• Intuition	(N)	• Perceiving	(P)

Favorite world: Do you prefer to focus on the outer world, or on your own inner world? Extraversion (E) vs. Introversion (I). ***Information:*** Do you prefer to focus on the basic information you take in, or do you prefer to interpret and add meaning? Sensing (S) vs. Intuition (N). ***Decisions:*** When making decisions, do you prefer to first look at logic and consistency, or first look at the people and special circumstances? Thinking (T) vs. Feeling (F). ***Structure:*** In dealing with the outside world, do you prefer to get things decided, or do you prefer to stay open to new information and options? Judging (J) vs. Perceiving (P).

HOW DO YOU PREFER TO TRANSACT?

- One-On-One
- Phone/Mobile
- Social Media
- Direct Mail
- Special Events
- Collateral Documents
- Email/Online
- Video/Streaming

"Orientations" is key to maximizing your participation. Finding out what makes you tick is an art form, and takes years of practice (thus the term "practitioner").

TRUST TRANSACTION...PERSONALITY
YOU LIKE THEM, THEY ENGAGE YOU GRACEFULLY

How do you want to be treated?

THE DAUGHTER I NEVER HAD BUT ALWAYS WANTED

I was speaking to a group of nonprofit radio broadcasters at Gospel Music Association's Dove Awards Week in Nashville. We were tackling major gifts fundraising and three or four people in the back row began grilling me on a myriad of topics. After the session was over, their energetic leader approached me with an extended hand and said, "Hi, my name's Victoria Hearst. You probably don't know me, but you may have heard of my grandfather, William, or my sister, Patty!"

Victoria Hearst is one of five remaining family heirs, who are the recipients of their legendary grandfather's publishing fortune.

She handed me her card and said, "Call me next week." Then she was off.

After a few phone conversations, I was on my way to Grand Junction, Colorado, to visit with Victoria at her mountain compound (she'd purchased actor Dennis Weaver's eco-ranch, and re-purposed its facilities to serve the at-risk youth of Colorado's Western Slope).

Upon my arrival, Lucretia Church, Director of Development, gave me a tour of the ranch. Lucretia had a winning smile and was engaging, gracious, and smart. Within the hour, she had seemingly (and without effort) convinced me that she was genuinely interested in all the fun things that were happening in my life, family, and work.

After the tour, Lucretia ushered me up to the second floor of McCloud's Saloon and Dance Hall, into a converted office, for my meeting with Ms.

Hearst. I walked in and gave my new friend a hug. Falling onto her couch, I settled in and said,

"Victoria…

…tell me everything."

For the next two hours, she poured out her heart, sharing a litany of opportunities, obstacles, accomplishments, and goals. I responded with a conversation about the role major gifts fundraising could play in expanding her ministry. I also let her know that her success or failure would in no small part be contingent on the staff she provided to implement our program.

Victoria didn't miss a beat and asked, "Have you met Lucretia?" I replied, "Yes, in Nashville, on the phone, and for the last hour touring your facilities."

She then asked, "What'd you think?"

I said, "She's inviting and fun…any donor would look forward to a visit from Lucretia…it would be the highlight of their day."

Victoria replied, *"She's the daughter I never had, but always wanted."*

We ended up serving Victoria for the next eighteen months, and with Lucretia's help, launched their first major gifts fundraising program.

I share that story because it's my belief that any visit by a fundraiser should end up feeling like you just sat down and enjoyed the all the fun that comes when eating a banana split! When I hear that my favorite development officer is on the phone, it's like someone just brought me dessert.

One day, Lucretia called me to check in and see how I was doing. I'm always moved by a person who takes time to let me know they care. I'm not sure that there's a greater gift in life than those moments when someone celebrates another. From time-to-time, I pay them the highest honor I know, sharing something like this:

"Lucretia…that was so much fun…thanks, pal…*you're a great development officer.*"

Lucretia responded:

"Jimmy, I'm not doing development…I was calling just to let you know that I was thinking of you."

Her genuine response made me wince. You see, the implication was that "development" is attached to something nefarious. I suppose what's ultimately being called into question is our "motives" as we attempt to engage you as a friend. Our acts of gratitude are confused with sales methods, moves management, or even worse...MANIPULATION.

Here are the facts. The consummate fundraiser provides you (the donor) an important service. Bill Gates recently said, *"Giving money effectively is almost as hard as earning it in the first place."* That's why a trustworthy fundraising practitioner, who is truly committed to a donor-driven philosophy, is a gift to you and the philanthropic community.

Giving money effectively is almost as hard as earning it in the first place. That's why the fundraising practitioner, who is truly committed to your interests is a gift to you and the philanthropic community.

Conclusion:

Here's my calling. I'm privileged to support philanthropists by connecting their personal investment decisions to great needs around the world. Good fundraisers ensure that your choice to release your finances transforms both you and those in whom you invest. Good practitioners serve donors by heeding Cotton Mather's charge to donors when he said, *"Instead of exhorting you to augment your charity, I will rather utter an exhortation, or at least a supplication, that you may not abuse your charity by misapplying it."*

RIP QUIZ #5

1. Have you ever had a spectacular giving experience? If so, why?

2. Have you ever had a bad giving experience? If so, why was it bad?

3. Respond to this statement: "YOU are a nonprofit's primary customer."

4. Do you like to be involved in the organizations to which you give? What kind of involvement works for you? What kind of involvement doesn't work for you?

5. Do you have goals for yourself, your family, your church and community that are accomplished through philanthropic giving? If so, name five outcomes you'd like to see happen when you make a meaningful gift.

6. Has a fundraiser ever taken the time to explore your personal goals?

9. Who is your favorite development officer? Describe the different reasons why he or she are your favorite.

THE METHOD

When I first started talking about running for office, a lot of people said to me, 'Don't let the consultants change you,' and I'd always assure them it would never happen. But like it or not, I had to listen to them, because I started to understand the cost of making stupid mistakes.

~Elizabeth Warren

THE POWER OF NONPROFIT CONSULTING

The purpose of RE-IMAGINING PHILANTHROPY is to empower you (the donor) to transform the sector so significantly that it affects great global change. We established in chapter one that you are uniquely positioned to influence this movement from your place of success, wisdom, and wealth.

One of the greatest tools in your arsenal to affect transformation is the consultant.

I am also of the conviction that, beyond your experiences, the greatest tool in your arsenal to affect transformation is *the nonprofit consultant.* Charities rely on this network of practitioners (there are thousands across the U.S., U.K., and Europe) for their proficiencies and vast reservoirs of knowledge. They, like you, are similarly positioned to supercharge the renovation of the sector. We must engage their hearts and minds, for their power over the healthcare, education, human welfare, arts, and environmental sectors is enormous. Here's the problem: *Consultants are one of the biggest reasons nonprofits are in this mess in the first place.*

Consultants are one of the primary reasons nonprofits are in this mess in the first place.

Consultants keep nonprofits in a state of paralysis by prescribing solutions that deal with symptoms, rather than healing the systemic issues (people, process, product, etc.).

Most are simply misguided and without malice. *Many know exactly what they are doing.*

Your influence is matched, even superseded at times, by practitioners who are blind to the realities of their profession. This chapter tackles this problem by *first, revealing facts they don't want you to know, and second, by providing you solutions they must embrace.*

In making these revelations, I will be charged with damaging the consulting profession. What I'm attempting to do is actually so much worse than that.

I don't want to "damage" the profession...*I want to "kill"* it in its present form, ushering in an era of resurrection, where thousands of practitioners RE-IMAGINE PHILANTHROPY in a way that changes the world.

This is a defining moment. Never has a finer group of professionals been positioned to affect such great change within such an important movement. The "change" I speak of will not be easy, as it can only be discovered in the fiery crucible of a "great repentance."

It will require consultants to stop charging charities millions of dollars for disproved methods that haven't worked in decades.

It will require consultants to stop charging charities millions of dollars for disproved methods that haven't worked in decades.

This massive shift will more easily be embraced by practitioners if *YOU FIRST DISRUPT THE FLOW OF MONEY FROM CHARITIES TO CONSULTANTS.*

I hope to inspire you to withdraw your funds, and instead use the resources you generously give to help nonprofits get well. Once the curtain is pulled back, and I show you what's really going on, your perspective will be forever changed.

"THERE WILL BE WAILING AND GREAT GNASHING OF TEETH!"

Both men and women alike will cry foul, foul, foul!!!

Regardless, the path I am about to propose ends with consultants being remunerated to help nonprofits, instead of hurt them.

We can do this.

FEASIBILITY STUDIES:
THE CRACK COCAINE OF NONPROFIT CONSULTING

Money for Nothing

~Mark Knopfler

As a reminder, here's the fundraising industry's explanation of a campaign feasibility study, as defined by consultant P. Burke Keegan:

> *A feasibility study is an objective survey of the community that assesses the likelihood of success for a fundraising project, and identifies strategies and specific individual givers for the campaign. A feasibility study can also be used to contemplate launching a new program, merging with another nonprofit, or taking a hard look at the effectiveness of the ways you do fundraising.*

> *If you as a board member were to ask others whether they would support a campaign, your friends might feel they need to be positive, so an independent consultant usually conducts individual private interviews with community leaders, prospective foundations and individual donors, and key friends (and enemies!) of your nonprofit. What you can learn by talking to people with history with the organization, and people with expertise in your field, may astound you.*

On the face of it, this definition makes sense and places a high value on the outcomes a feasibility study would likely supply. Why, then, have I titled this section *FEASIBILITY STUDIES: THE CRACK COCAINE OF NONPROFIT CONSULTING?*

See the response from a feasibility study consultant who heard about my section title.

*Regarding his use of the term 'crack cocaine,' the 'Kardashian Style'
direction Mr. LaRose has taken is not the answer. Rather than opening
the discussion to philanthropic consultants and sincerely promoting
stronger service to good causes, Mr. LaRose has chosen to insult the
integrity of philanthropic consulting with a superficial pop culture, self-
promoting broad brush. It is unfortunate...bottom line...ethics matter.*

The author infers that I'm violating professional standards by using
incendiary rhetoric for the sake of effect. What she has failed to recognize
is that *THE CHARITABLE SECTOR HAS AN ORGANIZED "DRUG
DEALER" AND "DRUG USER" PROBLEM*, rooted in a well-known secret
agreement between nonprofits and consultants.

The charitable sector has an organized "drug dealer" and "drug user" problem, rooted in a well-known (yet secret) agreement between nonprofits and consultants.

It goes something like this...

**We (nonprofits) will pay you (consultants) large sums of cash to perform
unhealthy acts of triangulation with our donors, because we're not
willing to do the important work of serving our supporters above client,
issue, or cause.**

Tragically, it is the very definition of addiction, for, like the "war on
drugs," and after decades of discussions about the "valuelessness" of
feasibility studies, charities continue to give consultants thousands of
dollars to perform them. The futility of this war metaphor is further
confirmed by the late Arthur C. Frantzreb, who wrote:

We (nonprofits) will pay you (consultants) large sums of cash to perform unhealthy acts of triangulation with our donors, because we're not willing to do the important work of serving our supporters above client or cause.

Perhaps 90 percent of such studies are conducted by consultants long before the organization is ready, which creates an attitude of expectancy that can be crucially counterproductive.

Art wrote an essay twenty years ago, revealing the damage consultants visit on nonprofits using feasibility studies. Despite his warnings, and like the "war on drugs," nothing has changed, as charities continue to spend your cash on a method that has proven itself ineffective.

(By the way, Art Frantzreb is one of the more celebrated consultants of the last century, and personally mentored my mentor of twenty years [I consider myself one of his many professional grandchildren…so to speak.])

Here's another comment from a feasibility study consultant (If you'll read closely, you'll see further confirmation of this conspiracy to triangulate.):

*The nonprofits we work with don't have the staff capacity to interview their donors before a campaign, nor the will to make it a priority. In fact, **we're cultivating their donors for them.** We could train their senior staff to conduct interviews, but most are not willing to invest the time and energy. Feasibility studies will continue to be necessary as long as nonprofits are unwilling to spend time with donors one-on-one.*

Executive directors who *"do not have the staff capacity to interview their donors,"* should be replaced with a chief executive officer (CEO) who understands that the homeless family they're serving IS NOT THEIR CUSTOMER (because they have no money), but rather YOU ARE THEIR CUSTOMER (because you have money), and are the true object of their nonprofit enterprise.

Remember the "corrected" mission statement we cited earlier?

> *Harvest Hope Food Bank provides donors, volunteers, and advocates the organization they require to support our community's hurting, hungry, and homeless.*

See yet another response below, from a professor at one of our most prominent American universities:

> *LaRose's declaration that feasibility studies are "a colossal waste of time" may get the attention of those who are predisposed to criticize charities, but…will likely do nothing to help nonprofits understand the nuances of how to best prepare for a campaign.*

It is so much worse than just *"a colossal waste of time."* Rather, it is like a greedy physician who builds his or her practice by doling out pain medications to nonprofits who would rather escape the discomfort of change, than do the harder work of actually getting well.

Why the vitriol? Simply because the revelations made in this section challenge the existing order of things

(that's code for…*I'm messing with someone's money*).

There will be a rash of consultants who will attempt to debunk what you are about to read by declaring, ETHICS, ETHICS, ETHICS!!! *They will insist that ETHICAL FUNDRAISERS would never engage in such behaviors.*

Here is the problem…They "doth protest too much."

My experiences are first person, and are not based on isolated encounters with unethical fundraisers. Rather, they have been formed after working with or near individuals from the most recognized firms in the U.S. and Europe for over a quarter of a century. I will quote them directly, though I doubt anyone will ask for specific names. These individuals know who they are, what they have said, and that what I'm about to reveal is the way they presently operate.

So let's first explore who's "dealing" this product in the first place.

Twenty-five years ago, I received my very first issue of the *Chronicle of Philanthropy*. It was an exciting publication, full of color photos, spectacular articles, and ads that greatly influenced my early years as a fundraising practitioner. After carefully reading every word, I turned it over, and on the back outside cover, saw a full page ad paid for by the now defunct Ketchum Company. Ketchum was the granddaddy of all fundraising consulting agencies, and spun off many of the firms that remain in practice today. They declared on a full back page ad, in big block letters…

"THE 'FEASIBILITY STUDY' IS DEAD"
THE KETCHUM COMPANY

Think about it. The very first time I ever saw the word "feasibility" as a new fundraiser, it was being de-positioned in the negative. I later discovered that Ketchum was attempting to re-brand studies as a cultivation tool, and no longer as a method whereby "feasibility" was determined.

Recently, the *Chronicle* featured an opinion piece authored by a "planning study" consultant, who opened his defense by sharing, *"Most of the consultants I know, including myself, stopped using the term "feasibility" years ago...We haven't used the 'f' word in at least two decades."*

He went on to explain that the term "campaign" or "planning" study was a better way to describe the important work a consultant does. His argument may have had some merit, until he revealed his personal evaluation of **thirty** separate *"planning studies"* performed by his firm. Here are what his *"planning studies"* revealed about the nonprofits he served:

1. 50% of the planning studies he performed indicated that the nonprofit had non-existent or poor strategic planning, disallowing the possibility of campaign (these facts should have halted the expense of a "study" before it even started.).

2. 50% of nonprofits dramatically miscalculated volunteer leaders' interest in participating in the campaign (which can be determined well in advance of the feasibility process).

3. 30% of potential donors were not interested in participating in a campaign interview (which bruises relationships with key supporters).

4. In several instances, the largest gifts made to the campaign were not uncovered by the planning study (which further demonstrates the ineffectiveness of "studies").

5. Quite often, unpredictable events had occurred BEFORE donors were interviewed (CEO departure, scandal, etc.), making the project untenable (which should have prevented monies from ever being spent on a study in the first place).

Calling "studies" by a different name changes nothing. With just one or two day's work, this consultant could have forecasted these same conclusions without having sold the nonprofit a four or five month feasibility study. What is worse is that consultants respond to RFPs knowing full well that the feasibility study they are about to sell will come back with a resounding report of "YOU'RE NOT READY."

They know this before they go on the marketing call.

They can't stop or help themselves because of an archaic business model upon which they rely for personal income. Again, I cite the previously mentioned consultant. His own data suggests half of the thirty studies performed were unnecessary, and would have deprived him of hundreds of thousands of dollars in revenue (By the way, before this chapter is over, I'll demonstrate how the other 50% he deemed "successful" were also a waste as well.).

Allow me to further pull back the curtain and share some well-known facts that consultants don't want you (the donor) to know about the "feasibility study racket."

EIGHT SECRETS CONSULTANTS DON'T WANT YOU TO KNOW ABOUT FEASIBILITY STUDIES

#1 - THE DYSFUNCTION OF TRIANGULATION

Consultants have convinced nonprofits that the "private interview" is not only priceless, but sacred. They will insist with great fervor that you (the donor) prefer the anonymity of a survey performed by an objective third party. They claim that you will be more transparent and share your true feelings. Here is a quote from a feasibility study consultant regarding anonymity:

*When study interviews are done with the **inviolable pledge of anonymity,** donors are truly free to share what they might give, and also express reservations about leadership or vision that they might not otherwise reveal for fear of damaging relationships.*

The number of things wrong with this statement are innumerable.

Major donors like yourself (who give five, six or seven figure gifts) share their concerns directly with leadership. Donors who make big gifts do not use a third party to reveal their secret anxieties. ***Feasibility study consultants brazenly sell the dysfunction of triangulation as one of the most important features of their product.***

Triangulation, by definition, is a situation in which one family member communicates indirectly with another through a third party. The concept originated in the study of unhealthy families, but can describe behaviors in other systems, including work and management.

Incidentally, triangulation is the most addictive aspect of this toxic "high". It cements the relationship between the dealer and the addict. The consultant promises the nonprofit they can reap the benefits of a relationship without having to actually be in one. Here's the truth about the "anonymous" third party interview...*it is a very powerful sales tactic.* For it promises, with the ease of "just-add-water," the impossible outcome of new dollars raised.

Simply put, triangulation is the enemy of intimacy, and has co-dependently fed the abnormality of nonprofit management for decades.

Triangulation is the enemy of intimacy and has co-dependently fed the abonormality of nonprofit management for decades

---

#2 - THE DECEPTION OF CONFIDENTIALITY

Feasibility study consultants will tell (or infer to) both the nonprofit and the interviewee that the meeting is being held in anonymity.

Here's a direct quote:

> *"Ultimately, outside counsel will always be needed to provide a donor the confidentiality they require to reveal their honest, unvarnished view of the organization and its vision."*

Here is the problem: the anecdotal information you provide during a "confidential interview" is shared word-for-word and in writing, even though it may not be attributed to you directly. I have seen a countless number of administrators and staff read through a feasibility study report and blurt out, "Well, we know who said that!" Furthermore, the gift amount you shared is not confidential, and ultimately makes its way into a future gift request.

When you are told that the interview is private, you're being manipulated. The consultant has been hired to gather information from you and disseminate it DIRECTLY to leadership.

#3 - LOOK AT ALL THE STARTLING REVELATIONS

I recently spoke with a consultant who shared, *"I recently finished up a series of interviews that revealed some real problems with the organization. The leadership had no idea!"* He suggested that the privacy of the interview played a key role in uncovering what was really going on. When a "feasibility study" comes back with some sort of "startling revelation" about leadership, a campaign, or the organization, it's an indication that the staff of the nonprofit failed to be in any real relationship with you in the first place. Simply put, it is the first time the right questions have ever been asked, NOT that the privacy of the interview made you feel safer.

Here's what you (the donor) have to say about this issue.

> *I've been the head of our foundation for twenty-five years. Virtually every capital campaign conducted during that time frame has hired a consultant to do a feasibility study. They've all met with me. After explaining their case, which I already knew, they ask where our gift might fit on their campaign chart. They also ask who I thought would be good leaders for their campaign, and who might make lead gifts. They also inquire as to my concerns about the project's success. For what it's worth, everything I say in those meetings, I would have said to the board or staff leadership directly, FOR FREE.*

Donors that make significant investments do so as result of trust, built on a foundation of shared values, not because a fundraising consultant provided them "anonymity."

#4 - USING A STUDY TO DETERMINE FUNDRAISING GOAL

Despite their desperate attempts to rebrand "feasibility studies" as a cultivation tool (rather than a method to see if a campaign is "feasible"), the consultant will still insist on how important it is to use the study to develop a realistic campaign goal. Here is what they say:
We use the study findings not only as an indicator of what the potential goal may be, but to also build a campaign calendar that reveals the time period in which campaign cash begins to offset costs. Planning studies should be seen as a way to determine the scale of the goal (not just if it's feasible to have a campaign).

Oh, the double talk! Let's bring some clarity to this issue by referencing Art Franztreb again.

We are well into an era of surveys, market testing, consumer pools, and philanthropic feasibility studies…though such studies can stimulate constructive criticism…they are unreliable indicators of realistic potential.

The big moment for me, the one that dramatically changed my beliefs regarding the value of feasibility studies, occurred during a campaign headed up by a chamber of commerce in a small rural town out in the Midwest. The board determined that their members' business interests would be best served by investing in the arts, and the most effective way to accomplish this goal would be to support an established nonprofit that happened to be in need of a new facility.

They also decided that a consultant should be hired to perform a feasibility study.

The consultant met with the volunteer campaign chair, who provided him forty-two names of individuals to be solicited. This gentleman was a well-heeled small business owner, who, over the decades, had built friendships with all the prominent families and leaders in town.

Upon completion of the study, the campaign chair met with the consultant and said, "Okay, give me the name of each person and the amount they thought they could give." Evidently, the issue of anonymity didn't come up, for the consultant immediately produced the written surveys. He got out a pad and wrote down each name and a dollar amount...twenty-seven in all.

(Watch what happens next to see how a "real campaign goal" is determined!)

The campaign chair took the pad and thoughtfully read out loud the name that had been written at the top of the list and their proposed gift amount. He then wrote a new number next to the entry. He went on and read the second prospect's name and their proposed gift amount, and once again wrote down a new number. He repeated this process twenty-seven times and then asked, "Where are the other fifteen?" The consultant replied, "They weren't available to meet." The chair replied, "Okay, that's alright, give me their names." The consultant asked for his pad back and wrote down the fifteen remaining names. The chair took the list and wrote, yet again, a number next to each name, and then thanked the consultant, saying, "You did a great job, but I'm not sure you needed to interview these folks."

Here's what he did. He took the initial list of twenty-seven interviewees, and wrote down a new dollar amount he knew each family could give. He was confident in his own personal knowledge that they would participate at a higher level. Some will say he couldn't have done that without the initial interview. Well, he then took the remaining fifteen (who were never interviewed) and wrote down dollar amounts for each. Ultimately, two of the largest gifts made to the campaign came from the list of fifteen.

He then went ahead and asked six friends to perform visits with his forty-two prospects. He told them to feel free to use his name, and the following line during the solicitation:

> *"Dave Holmes thought your family would be willing to partner with the chamber on this project with a gift of $50,000."*

The gifts Dave and his team of visitors raised exceeded the feasibility study findings by 50%, and the campaign goal by 26%.

Witness the anatomy of a perfect capital campaign, in which the "goal" was determined through the natural constructs of friendship.

FEASIBILITY STUDY CONSULTANTS WILL CRY, "THAT'S NOT FAIR…THE VAST MAJORITY OF NONPROFITS DON'T HAVE A CAMPAIGN CHAIR WITH THOSE SKILL SETS OR BEVY OF RELATIONSHIPS."

I would respond by asking, *"You mean you'd actually perform a feasibility study before identifying a skilled campaign chair who possesses a bevy of relationships?"* and, "By the way, how does your forty-five minute feasibility study interview solve the enormous problem of not having a campaign chair?"

Neither "campaign goals," nor the "chairpersons" who help determine them are identified in a feasibility study interview. This task falls to well-cultivated friends who have been meaningfully involved, and reveals whose turn it is to ensure campaign success.

#5 FEASIBILITY STUDIES ARE SOLD TO NONPROFITS THAT DON'T NEED THEM (AND NEVER WILL)

The problem with this point is the underlying assumption that THERE ACTUALLY ARE some nonprofits that *could* benefit from a feasibility study. Remember Art Franztreb's statement, "90% are not ready." His words could infer that 10% ARE READY, and that the remaining 90% COULD BE at some future point. However, if you read his work, you will discover that he developed methods that eliminated his use of feasibility studies as a tool.

Here is the rub. Even if you are able to somehow justify letting consultants cultivate your donors (which you can't), consultants still sell this product to thousands of nonprofits…

> …who haven't developed a strategic plan
> …who aren't unified around a case for support
> …who don't have relationships with prospects to be interviewed
> …who are run by a weak board of directors
> …who have been destabilized by scandal or administrative departures
> …who etc. etc. etc.

CONSULTANTS WILL CRY "THAT'S NOT FAIR!!!"

WE PERFORM CAMPAIGN STUDIES FOR SOLID ORGANIZATIONS LIKE UNIVERSITIES AND HOSPITALS WHO NOT ONLY BENEFIT FROM THEM, BUT CAN AFFORD THEM AS WELL."

Large institutions flitter away funds more than most. In fact, because they're well-funded, they waste these monies on studies with little or no financial consequence.

So, if you're supporting a university president, and she is considering the value of a feasibility study, remind her that Princeton exceeded a $350 million dollar campaign goal without ever using a third party to interview their donors.

If you're working with a hospital CEO who is going to hire a consultant to perform a "planning study," stop them! The proper "NO" decision will prevent thousands of your dollars from *being spent on an overpriced "hit-and-run" tactic that adds no long term value to the institution*. Instead, make sure those funds are used to hire more field officers to build meaningful friendships with the families who financially underwrite the hospital's mission.

#6 - ETHICS, ETHICS, ETHICS, ETHICS

In response to RE-IMAGINING PHILANTHROPY, a leading planning study consultant wrote the following:

*The consultants I know subscribe to the rules of ethical conduct established by the Giving Institute or by the Association of Fundraising Professionals' Code of Ethical Standards. The obligation always to act ethically is a **powerful disinfectant** and removes the taint of conflict...*

Powerful disinfectant? Evidently not! Ethics are subjective, and easily swept away when an entire industry is relying on a business model that generates personal income. Money (in spite of ethics) is the reason why 90% of nonprofits (Franztreb used that number, not me) are being sold a product that does not work.

Regarding the "codes" established by The Giving Institute or Association of Fundraising Professionals: there's NOT ONE WORD regarding the buying or selling of "feasibility studies" (despite decades of controversy).

I once met with a regional board of directors who oversaw their denomination's year-round camping and retreat facility. One of their veteran members was a feasibility study consultant, from a large consulting firm that performed studies and provided campaign support. Though this meeting was out of state, we were both members of the same chapter of the Association of Fundraising Professionals. Over the years, we had admired one another's work from a distance.

Their board had come together to spend two days wrestling through a new strategic plan. Upon completion of the first day's work, we meandered over to their dining hall for some dinner. At some point during the evening, the conversation turned to other nonprofits and what "was" and "wasn't" working. My fellow AFP chapter member (whose entire cadre of fellow-consultants were also AFP members) then shared the dark realities his firm engaged in when performing a feasibility study.

He blurted out, "The truth is, the unwritten policy at our firm is to write every 'report' in a way that leads to the earliest possible start date."

I asked, "So, how many reports return a 'not ready' finding?"

He replied, **"None."**

I then asked, "How many organizations are *actually* ready?"

He hesitated, and then glibly replied, **"Hardly any."**

I went ahead and confirmed what I thought I was hearing. "So, let me get this straight. You're saying that every study report your consultants write comes back with some sort of finding that leads to more paid work?"

He replied, "Hey, I know it's not right, but it's the way we pay the bills."

CONSULTANTS WILL CRY…

"FIRMS LIKE THAT DON'T LAST…THE MARKETPLACE TAKES CARE OF BAD BEHAVIOR THAT'S UNETHICAL."

The incident I shared above took place seven years ago. Since that time, *that same firm has expanded, adding new consultants, despite the failed campaigns that followed.*

CONSULTANTS WILL CRY...

"THAT'S NOT FAIR!!! JUST BECAUSE SOME ARE UNETHICAL DOESN'T MEAN WE'RE ALL UNETHICAL!"

Here's a response from a consultant regarding the concerns I've outlined about ethics in RE-IMAGINING PHILANTHROPY:

> *Are there still consultants out there who inflate the potential for a campaign in their study to get the consulting gig? Are there doctors who order unnecessary tests? If Mr. LaRose was serious about his professed concerns, he would be helping nonprofits research the integrity of their prospective consultants, not just shouting "crack cocaine!" or "the emperor has no clothes!"*

(By the way, this "drug metaphor" thing has really worked. I've never had this many naked people try to convince themselves [in writing] that their "invisible coat" was so much prettier than everyone else's.)

Here's the problem with the *"doctors who order unnecessary tests"* comment. In the world of nonprofits...IF the physician (fundraising consultant) who's already been paid $25,000 to diagnosis (feasibility study) the patient's readiness to run a marathon (upcoming campaign), declares the runner fit to race, the physician is THEN rewarded with additional work that pays $100,000, $200,000 even $500,000 in fees as a consultant to the race team. *The temptation is too powerful.*

Here's what a study consultant wrote after reading about my concerns:

I have to take issue with this notion of consultants being "prejudiced" because they may do the campaign implementation. I can't think of a single study I've ever conducted where the assumption wasn't that—assuming favorable findings—I wouldn't be involved in the execution of the campaign. The real issue, I think, is whether the consultant's desperation of a consulting engagement clouds their judgement. But that's a failure of the consultant, not the study process.

If you read his comment closely, he makes my point. I've seen too many "judgements clouded" by the monies that stand to be made if a favorable finding is reached.

Hey, even cocaine has a few "ethical" applications (e.g., numbing the cornea for optic surgery, etc.). However, its disadvantages and powerful temptations far outweigh any of its value when used by the masses.

When it comes to feasibility studies, I'm begging you to THROW THE BABY OUT WITH THE BATH WATER. Stop participating in them. Throw them out...baby and all (including the "powerful disinfectant" of ethics!).

#7 - FEASIBILITY STUDIES ARE GREAT WAY TO CULTIVATE

As cited earlier, consultants began re-branding "feasibility studies" years ago as part of the cultivation process. They suggested that a "study" can be a device that allows nonprofits to bring donors into a campaign early, providing them an opportunity to own and shape the vision. Here's what they say:

Campaign planning builds ownership among constituents and allows an objective third-party, i.e., an experienced consultant, to engage the donor. The planning process gives us a chance to nudge major prospects to higher levels and in many cases stimulates a first gift.

You see, the feasibility study interview is one of many steps used to lead you to a "yes" decision regarding your personal gift investment. In many cases, the actual "questionnaire" itself is designed to systematically move you towards a "yes" response. This is not "donor cultivation," rather it's "donor manipulation," and is made worse by the use of the word "private" or "anonymous."

What about all this talk about how important it is to engage you using a feasibility study? Trust me, it's just another sales tactic. Think about it. How does a single forty-five minute interview (performed by a person you'll likely never see again) help build a meaningful relationship with you and your family?

IT DOESN'T!!!

Here's what you have to say:

My family gave me the responsibility for properly investing our wealth in causes that are meaningful to our community. Regarding feasibility studies…it reminds me of a 1970s book title I loved: if you meet Buddha on the road, kill him. ***If you meet a feasibility study from an outsider, run***. *The most passionate, committed insiders, with skill and a great case for support, are the only qualified people to cultivate prospects for campaign.*

#8 - NONPROFITS DON'T HAVE THE TIME TO CULTIVATE

Believe it or not, the consultant is the lesser of two evils in this equation. Or, as one of my professors in college insisted on saying, *"The evil of two lessers!"*

The real problem is with nonprofit administrators, staff, and boards!

Charities who conduct third-party interviews view you (their donors) as Automatic Teller Machines that exist somewhere outside the organization. They believe you can be visited by a third-party hack, who promises to "drive thru" and extract as many of your dollars as possible using some sort of MAGIC PIN NUMBER.

Please remember the consultant's quote I shared earlier,

*The nonprofits we work with don't have the staff capacity to interview their donors before a campaign, nor the will to make it a priority. In fact, **we're cultivating their donors for them.** We could train their senior staff to conduct interviews, but most are not willing to invest the time and energy. Feasibility studies will continue to be necessary as long as nonprofits are unwilling to spend time with donors one-on-one.*

(By the way, have you noticed [from reading all these comments] how many consultants still call feasibility studies…feasibility studies?)

The failure of nonprofits to sustain themselves was explored earlier in RE-IMAGINING PHILANTHROPY, when I asserted that nonprofits **mistakenly** believe that their mission is to serve a certain population, protect an environment, or advance a cause. *We established that you, the donor, are the true customers of nonprofit enterprise (because you have money), not clients or causes (because they have no money).* You'll also remember the way I contrasted correct and incorrect mission statements. Remember the typical (incorrect) mission statement:

> *Harvest Town Food Bank exists to provide our community's hurting, hungry, and homeless the clothing, food, and nutritional care they so desperately need.*

Here is a proper (correct) example:

> *Harvest Town Food Bank provides donors, volunteers, and advocates the organization they require to support our city's hurting, hungry, and homeless.*

You see, charities that commit to true nonprofit enterprise hire a CEO who understands that their chief responsibility is to generate revenue. Good CEOs retool their organization by firing program staff, and using those freed up funds to hire fundraising staff. They do this because they know that their true program revolves around serving people who financially invest in clients and causes and who care about civil society.

What's the first right step a good CEO takes to advance their nonprofit's enterprise? ***THEY HIRE A CONSULTANT!!!***

SUPER CONSULTANTS WHO TRANSFORM NONPROFITS

Three years ago, I was invited by a friend to sit in on a board meeting for a private school. This full day gathering had been called by the board chair, based on the recommendation of the school principal. In a previous position, the principal enjoyed the benefits of a robust fundraising program. They'd determined that by inviting different consulting firms to present their wares, the school board would experience a thorough orientation to the art of fundraising.

Each firm was provided the same set of data, which concisely overviewed the institution's history, student body size, alumni count, etc. Each firm knew that the school had never implemented a fundraising program, and relied solely on tuition to pay the bills. *One of the consultants represented the largest and most respected campaign fundraising firms in the Southeast.*

Two of the three presenters thoroughly overviewed the importance of performing a feasibility study. The big firm proposed a $10,000 per month engagement, to include both an internal and external campaign readiness audit. For the internal portion, administrators, staff, and board would meet with the consultant. For the external portion, fifty to seventy-five interviews would be performed by the consultant with key parents, grandparents, and alumni. The process would take approximately four months to complete.

After a very thorough and professional presentation, he invited each board member to share comments and questions.

Since this was the first time school leadership had ever considered "doing fundraising," a certain purity of inquiry emerged from the young families serving on the board. Questions like, "You mean YOU are going to meet with our families?" Someone said, "I'm not sure that would work here. We've never done fundraising before." Yet another queried, "Do you really think we're ready for something like this?"

The consultant, in a somewhat parental but gentle tone, once again explained how a feasibility study would be used to engage their families in a future fundraising effort.

The members were still a bit stumped as to how it all was supposed to work, and asked a series of uneducated questions that finally ended with the consulting saying,

"TRUST ME...YOU NEED TO DO A FEASIBILITY STUDY."

He was a "one-note-Johnny," who, despite his talk of board training, case development, and campaign planning, couldn't stop selling his product.

His proposed course of action was further confirmed by the second presenter, who further educated these members regarding the importance of performing a study.

SOME CONSULTANTS WILL CRY "FOUL," AND DECLARE, "OUR FIRM WOULD NEVER SUGGEST A FEASIBILTY STUDY IN THOSE CIRCUMSTANCES."

Here's the problem: TWO FIRMS OUT OF THREE DID, and one of them was one of the largest in the United States. Here's why...

...FEASIBILITY STUDIES ARE QUICK MONEY...QUICK and BIG.

The board instinctively declined the feasibility consultant offers, and opted not to conduct a feasibility study at all. The trustees reasoned that paying a stranger $40,000 to spend two or three days a month meeting with their families was illogical. They decided to do "something else," and, three years later, walked onto the stage of their new fine arts center, having raised every dollar philanthropically.

Here's what they did.

THEY HIRED THE THIRD CONSULTANT!

This seasoned veteran opened with, "I'm here to help you raise the monies you need in a way that's right for you and your constituents." He went on for a few minutes, and then someone blurted out, "What about a feasibility study?"

He replied, "You may have learned about feasibility studies from my colleagues who presented earlier, but the truth is we avoid those methods."

He went on, "After reading through the information you provided, I recommend that we take the monies you'd spend on a feasibility study and instead use the next three months to write a fundraising plan that fits your culture. I'd also suggest that, concurrently, we begin the process of hiring a full time fundraiser to implement the plan."

He then said, "None of this is rocket science. *We just need the right plan and the right person to implement it.*"

One board member queried, "What does a 'right plan' look like?" Someone else quickly asked, "What does a 'right person' look like?"

He said, "Here, I'll show you," and passed out a two page overview.

(At this point, I'm going to provide you a five-page overview that contrasts the first and second company's feasibility study offering with the third consultant's fundraising plan.)

I'm now going to provide you a multi-page review that contrasts Consultants #1 and #2 product offerings with Consultant #3.

FEASIBILITY STUDY MODEL vs MAJOR GIFTS RAMP-UP MODEL

FEASIBILITY STUDY MODEL (Consultants #1 & #2)

THE STATUS QUO - Board/Committee/Executive...

...May or MAY NOT have...committed to donors over clients or cause
...May or MAY NOT have...performed organizational development
...May or MAY NOT have...established strong case for support
...May or MAY NOT have...developed a written a fundraising plan

BUT WE THINK WE NEED MORE MONEY SO...

STEP #1 Hire consultant to perform feasibility study interviews

1. Report Comes Back...You're Not Ready (STOP)
2. Report Comes Back...You're Barely Ready (move on to STEP #2)
3. Report Comes Back...You're Ready (move on to STEP #2)

STEP #2 Hires same consultant to run campaign

1. Adjust Case for Support (based on feasibilty study)
2. Adjust Gift Range Chart (based on feasibilty study)
3. Write Campaign Cabinet Proposals (based on feasbility study)
4. Write Lead Gift Proposals (determine amounts as revealed by study)

STEP #3 Silent Phase

1. Establish Campaign Cabinet
2. Secure Lead Gifts

STEP #4 Public Phase

1. Volunteers Solicit Major Gifts
2. Staff Solict Other Gifts

OUTCOMES

1. Possibility of No Campaign
2. Possibility of Failed Campaign
3. Possibility of Stalled Campaign
4. Possibility of Successful Campaign (30%)

This list of uncertainties originates with feasibility studies of which, 70% result in no campaign, failed campaign OR stalled campaign. ***Feasibility study consultant gets paid either way (plus more to run a campaign that may stall or fail)***

(In truth, the remaining 30% of feasibility studies deemed "successful" came back positive because the organization had done the work long before the consultant got there)

MAJOR GIFTS RAMP-UP MODEL (Consultant #3)

STEP #1 Board makes a commitment to nonprofit enterprise

1. Money is more important than mission
2. Donors are more important than clients or causes
3. Monies reserved for feasibility study are now invested in hiring in-house development staff
4. If necessary cut programs to free up more cash to build additional in-house fundraising structures
5. If necessary spend freed up monies on hiring a real CEO (not an Executive Director)

STEP #2 Perform Institution-wide Organizational Development (OD)

1. Discover what the nonprofit truly needs to expand its mission
2. Determine operations, projects & endowment fundraising goals
3. What's "feasible" or "the cost" becomes irrelevant
4. Phase Goals - 5 years, 7 years, 10 years

STEP #3 Write five year fundraising plan for operations, one-time projects and endowment goal

1. Determine how new & existing prospects will be researched
2. Determine process whereby which prospects will be cultivated
3. Write comprehensive advancement calendar
4. Create campaign gift range chart

STEP #4 Develop compelling case for support based organizational development and written fundraising plan

There will always be generous people (you, the donor) who will amply support a GREAT DREAM backed by a SOUND PLAN

STEP #5 Prospect Identification (300 NEW & EXISTING)

1. Determine where the wealth set begins and ends (wide net)
2. Research existing & potential friends using online search tools
3. Identify ALL Campaign Chair & Co-Chair Prospects
4. Identify ALL Campaign Cabinet Prospects
5. Identify ALL Leadership Gift Prospects
6. Identify ALL Major Gift Prospects
7. Identify ALL Corporate Gift Prospects
8. Identify ALL Foundation Gift Prospects

STEP #6 Introduce prospects to case for support

TIME, MONIES & STAFF RESOURCES PREVIOUSLY SPENT ON WRESTLING UNCULTIVATED PROSPECTS INTO FEASIBILITY STUDY ARE NOW INVESTED IN CULTIVATNG PROSPECTS WITH PROPRIETY & GRACE

1. Create cultivation systems for each prospect - Individual Plans of Care (IPOC) consisting of Multiple Points of Contacts (MPOC)
2. Host non-fundraising "awareness events" for individuals, corporations, foundations inspiring them via Case for Support
3. Use existing fundraising & program events to introduce Case
4. Make individual calls to relationship build, explore interest and potential gift amounts
5. Use IPOCs to cultivate Campaign Cabinet Prospects (via MPOCs)
6. Use IPOCs to cultivate Leadership Gift Prospects (via MPOCs)
7. Use IPOCs to cultivate Major Gift Prospects (via MPOCs)
8. Use IPOCs to cultivate Corporate Gift Prospects (via MPOCs)
9. Use IPOCs to cultivate Foundation Gift Prospects (via MPOCs)
10. Use IPOCs to cultivate & solicit campaign chair (via MPOCs)

150 PROSPECTS IN PROCESS (EXISTING & NEW)

STEP #7 Activate Campaign Chair(s) & Cabinet Members

CABINET & STAFF MEANINGFULLY ENGAGE PROSPECTS TO
UNDERSTAND DONOR's GOALS & DETERMINE ASK AMOUNT

80 PROSPECTS IN PROCESS

1. Staff/Campaign Chair selects & solicits Co-Chair(s)
2. Staff/Campaign Chair & Co-Chair(s) solicits Cabinet Members
3. Staff/Cabinet adjusts/finalizes Case for Support
4. Staff/Cabinet adjusts Gift Range Chart
5. Cabinet secures their own personal gift investments
   (operations, projects & endowment)
6. Cabinet secures personal gift investments
   (operations, projects & endowment)
7. Cabinet finalizes list of FULLY CULTIVATED PROSPECTS
8. Continue to make individual calls to relationship build, explore interest and potential gift amounts
9. Cabinet based on their own knowledge, staff cultivation and research determine "ask" amounts for each prospect
   a. Determine smaller multi-year sustained gift for OPERATIONS
   b. Determine one time "stretch-gift" request for PROJECTS
   c. Determine how prospect could make a planned ENDOWMENT
10. Cabinet determines strongest linkages and divides solicitation among cabinet members & staff (only seven per member)
11. Cabinet determines solicitation calendar including progress reporting
12. If needed, Cabinet is trained and role plays in preparation for solicitation visits

STEP #8 Solicitation using the "Three-Part Ask""

1. Staff mails case for support & letter to finalized prospects list indicating their friend (cabinet member) will be calling
2. Staff creates visitors package for each prospect including custom Gift Prospectus, Case for Support & Gift Agreement
3. Cabinet Member sets appointments for each of their seven prospects
4. Cabinet Member with CEO (or staff member) make FORMAL VISIT to make FORMAL SOLICITATION
    a. Invite prospect to partner with a multi-year gift for OPERATIONS
    b. Invite prospect to make a "stretch-gift" to PROJECTS
    c. Invite prospect to make a planned gift for ENDOWMENT

40 GIFTS TO REACH GOAL

The school board took the monies they would have spent on a study, and combined it with a small portion of finances they would have spent on future campaign counsel. They then retained the third consultant for a significantly smaller amount per month (and, in case you're wondering, not me), to design and implement a sustainable fundraising program.

The consultant then hired their first PHILANTHROPY DIRECTOR who, with elegance, propriety, and grace, inspired their families to participate with financial gifts to an annual fund, capital projects, and endowment.

By the way…THEIR NEW PHILANTHROPY DIRECTOR WAS REALLY GOOD! You know what her secret was? *She took the time to get alone with each family to find out what made them tick.*

She took the time to get alone with each family to find out what made them tick.

She built trust. She celebrated their children. Over a period of months, she earned the right to "ask." Only then, after a meaningful relationship had been established, did she write a specific proposal designed to meet the unique needs of each family. On a case-by-case basis, she invited every household to become involved in a way that worked for them.

You see, the school board wisely avoided the waste of a planning/campaign/feasibility study. They invested their time and money in resources for building strong relationships with the moms, dads, and grandparents of the children they served.

They did not buy into the deception that hiring an outside consultant to meet with their families (for what, at best, may be a 45 minute interview) would have any real short or long-term value. In their naivety, they even wondered if this feasibility study product would hamper their effort, rather than help it.

Months later, I was at a conference with the consultant from the big firm. I updated him on the project. He shared, "Yeah, I got with our owner after that, to discuss cultivation strategies in advance of a study. The owner replied, 'What do you mean cultivation? Campaign interviews ARE our cultivation strategy.'"

CONSULTING...A NEW AGENDA

I have written RE-IMAGINING PHILANTHROPY to inspire you to champion a radical enterprise model that forces charities to *create the space they need to build financial sustainability.*

Simply put, NONPROFITS ARE BUSINESSES who, like any other business, prioritize the making of money to operate effectively.

The tenants of this enterprise model could include:

- Money is more important than mission (or ministry)
- Money is oxygen…without it, charities can't breathe
- Donors are more important than clients or causes
- Increased overhead is the key to nonprofit success
- Nonprofits don't need executive directors (they need CEOs)
- Volunteer boards don't work (it's OK…they don't have to)
- Make your CEO board chairman (it's OK…she already is)
- Board members don't fundraise (campaign cabinet members do)
- Consultants must STOP hurting and START healing the sector

You see, consultants are uniquely positioned to assist you with this movement, but instead have a proven record of making certain nonprofits "never become whole." I'm imploring you to end their distribution of toxic prescriptions, whose value expired long ago and serve only to keep charities in a perpetual state of frailty and ineffectiveness. We have been on this merry-go-round so long that *we've failed to recognize the solutions presently offered are the same elucidations that made us sick in the first place.*

It is the very definition of addiction.

These "offerings" are overpriced and have clever names, like…Board Training, Strategic Planning, Feasibility Studies, and Campaign Counsel. THEY ARE ACTIVITIES WITHOUT POWER, readily consumed by executives and boards desperate to demonstrate a form of flaccid "goings-on" *in place of transformational leadership that re-imagines philanthropy and changes everything!*

CONSULTANTS WILL CRY, "FOUL, FOUL, FOUL…BOARD TRAINING, STRATEGIC PLANNING, and FEASIBLITY STUDIES ARE VALUABLE SERVICES."

Really?

Why then, after four decades of board training, strategic planning, and feasibility studies, has the nonprofit sector remained a "non-growth" sector, leaving in its wake millions of people in need, untouched, and without life worth living?

Conclusion:

Donors must require consultants to write a new service manifesto based on training, planning, and consulting products that radically defy the existing order of things. Practitioners must lead charities through dramatic re-configuration, instituting programs that ensure long-term success, based on sound enterprise principals.

We've got to change. RE-IMAGINING PHILANTHROPY is the place consultants need to start.

RIP QUIZ #6

1. Have you ever participated in a feasibility study interview? If yes, describe your experience.

2. Have you ever been responsible for hiring a feasibility study consultant? In retrospect, was it the right way or wrong way to proceed? If it was the right way, explain why. If it was the wrong way, explain why.

3. Respond to this statement: "Nonprofits who hire consultants to meet with donors are involved in unhealthy acts of triangulation."

4. How much money have you seen a charity spend on a feasibility study?

5. Have you ever worked with a nonprofit consultant who was really good? If so, what did you like about them?

THE MODEL

Everything must be made as simple as possible. But not simpler.

~Albert Einstein

Let's end RE-IMAGINING PHILANTHROPY with a story that brings together all the "big ideas" we've been sorting through these past few hours. It's a story about a family of philanthropists, a strong CEO, and a SUPER CONSULTANT who proved the maxims found in this book long before I wrote about them. See if you can spot the different places where MOTIVE, MOVEMENT, MONEY, MANAGEMENT, MEANS, METHODS & MODELS emerge throughout this final narrative.

It starts with Jerry Strickland, patriarch and founder of the Jerry & Linda Strickland Family Foundation. Jerry's success in the energy business led to the creation of a family foundation directed by his wife, children, grandchildren, and nieces (over twenty family members to date), charged with investing their philanthropy in a manner that creates sustainability for nonprofits.

Jerry is all about "turnarounds," which (in his book of the same name) he defines as, *"Shorthand for the complex, dirty, dangerous job of oil refinery maintenance."* He expands on the "turnaround" concept by sharing:

"Each 'turnaround' is an intense experience, workers disassembling the heavy viscera of a refinery, repairing and updating it and then putting it all back together in a way that ensures increased production."

You see, the Strickland Family Foundation performs "turnarounds" for the nonprofits in which they financially invest. This family leads a nonprofit enterprise MOVEMENT that has placed MANAGEMENT, MONEY, MEANS, METHODS & MODELS in proper perspective.

My first encounter with the Strickland Family began at a fundraising conference. Here were the players:

Carter Strickland   (Philanthropist)
Strickland Family Foundation

Laura Whitaker   (Executive Director)
Extra Special People

Aimee Vance   (Consultant)
National Development Institute

I was speaking in Georgia at Gainesville State College for a National Development Institute Major Gifts Ramp-Up Conference, when in walked a young lady in her early twenties. She sat down in the front, took her "table-tent" out of her conference packet, and placed it in front of her, revealing her name, title, and organization.

Laura Whitaker
Executive Director
Extra Special People

About an hour into the workshop series, she thoughtfully engaged Aimee Vance, one of our veteran faculty members, asking for clarification on some of the big ideas you've read about in this book. I was up next, and at the end of my first session (I always ask for comments, questions, and pushback from the audience) Laura inquired,

"So what you're saying is that I need to prioritize supporting our donors as much as I do the children we serve?"

"Yep, you got it!" I replied.

She thought for a moment, and then said, *"I think I'm already doing that."*

I wasn't going to take her declaration lightly, so I, too, thought about it for a moment, and then asked, "Okay, so what does the phrase *'prioritize supporting donors'* mean to you?"

She thought about it for a second, and then responded with,

"My name is Laura Whitaker, and I'm the executive director at Extra Special People. We call ourselves ESP for short!"

(I resisted asking how old she was. Executive director? She seemed entirely too young.)

She went on, "We serve our children once a month on 'Flag Friday' with a full day of programs for families tackling developmental disabilities. During the summer, we host six weeks of camp for these same families. Otherwise, I spend every week making new friends with community leaders, sharing with them the good news of Extra Special People. The most important part of my job is to ensure everyone knows what we do. What's even more exciting is I have the privilege of providing new friends meaningful experiences with both our families and kids!"

She summed it up with, "I spend my days speaking for those who can't speak for themselves."

I looked to the audience and reverentially declared, *"Out of the mouths of babes and children…"* (Psalms 8:2)

Extra Special People (ESP) was founded years earlier in Athens, GA by Martha Wyllie, who had a passion for children with special needs. She believed young people needed a safe place where their families could focus on their *abilities*, instead of their *disabilities*. Martha grew ESP's program to 130 children, peaking right at $150,000 per year in revenue. She also acquired a small facility, where children could be served on-site. Martha died in 2004, and, of course, because of her passing, ESP was in danger of having to permanently shut its doors due to funding. Laura Whitaker, an eighteen year old ESP volunteer, rose to the occasion, inspiring both ESP families and the Athens community to save this program, raising $50,000 for immediate expenses. Soon after, in a bold move, Martha's remaining family members appointed <u>Laura to the position of executive director.</u>

(I've trained over 10,000 charities in my 25 years. Laura still holds the record for youngest person ever installed to executive director at an established nonprofit.)

Upon Martha's passing and Laura's subsequent installation as executive director, the Strickland Family Foundation saw the opportunity to perform a "turnaround!"

Now, back to the Major Gifts Ramp-Up Conference.

Our training events generally last two to three days, so during that time, Laura became fast friends with Aimee Vance. Aimee is an accomplished practitioner, and was one of my first clients in the early 90s. We were both in our twenties back then, and have spent a quarter of a century growing up together in the world of nonprofit management. At some point, we joined forces, and now Aimee builds Major Gifts Ramp-Up programs for charities across the U.S.

Laura told Aimee, "We need to do Major Gifts Ramp-Up at ESP." Aimee inquired, "Tell me about your board."

She replied, "Aww…I love my board. It's a small one, but each member knows exactly what they're doing. They work hard, and make sure I have what I need to succeed."

Aimee followed with, "What can you tell me about your donors?" Laura thought about it for a second, and said, "Well, my biggest donor is also a board member. *His name is Carter Strickland.*"

Jerry and Linda Strickland's children, Chip, Carter, Patia, Whitney, and Steve, were all taught the joy of giving from a very young age (long before Jerry accumulated his wealth). Carter serves as a trustee on the Strickland Family Foundation Board, and upon learning about Laura and ESP, brought this project back to the family.

For the record, the Strickland Family Foundation invests in nonprofits…

> …whose missions are clear
> …whose outcomes are measurable
> …who are led by strong administrators
> …who are generally smaller in size
> …who have great potential

Now, back to Laura.

After the conference, Laura went back to Carter and ESP's board to overview her Major Gifts Ramp-Up experience. She summed it up by saying, *"By the time the conference was over, fundraising finally made sense to me.* I now have a plan that will raise the funds we need to make budget this year."

Carter inquired, "So, what's your fundraising goal?" She was prepared and shared, "I've been working on our "case for support," and will be asking the board for approval to increase ESP's annual income from $190,000 per year to $600,000, while simultaneously launching a $3 million campaign for new facility acquisition and endowment."

The board collectively gasped. Carter said, "Wow...ok...we're with you... what kind of support do you need?" Again, Laura was ready, "I'd like to invite Jimmy LaRose and Aimee Vance from National Development Institute to meet with you. I think now's the right time for all of us to figure out how we can make Major Gifts Ramp-Up work here in Athens."

Two weeks later, Aimee, Laura, Carter, the ESP Board, and I gathered for an evening to explore ESP's future and the Major Gifts Ramp-Up model.

I started with, "Here's the good news. First, Laura is already spending a significant portion of her time building capacity. If she's going to increase annual fund, underwrite facilities, and build endowment, she'll have to remain in that mode. Second, Laura is a strong executive director, with a vision to grow ESP in a community that enjoys her. Simply put, people love Laura. Third, she feels supported by you, her board members, which has made her fearless as to what she thinks she can accomplish."

One member commented with a smile, "Well, we already knew that."

I replied, "Here's the better news. Laura's commitment to build capacity, combined with her relational skills plus your support, will ensure we reach goal!"

Another member queried, "What goal are you talking about?"

I replied, "Laura's bold fundraising goal, that increases ESP's annual fund by 220%, plus $3 million for one-time projects and endowment!"

He replied with a smile, "Oh yeah...that goal."

He then said, "$3 million dollars is a lot of money for a nonprofit with an annual budget of $190,000. Shouldn't we do a feasibility study first?"

I replied, "Well, we could, but all we'll discover is that the community doesn't know us well enough to offer any real opinions. We'll end up spending a lot of money to find out what we already know...*we're not ready*. That's why we do Major Gifts Ramp-Up."

To my relief, the group collectively murmured in agreement.

Carter then graciously shared, "The Strickland Family Foundation will underwrite the costs of National Development Institute's Major Gift Ramp-Up Campaign Program. *Let's provide Laura the support she needs to tackle this thing.*"

A few weeks later, Carter shared Laura's progress with his family. Jerry considered Carter's report, and began making plans to give ESP his largest gift ever. He believed what Laura really needed was a salary increase, additional administrative help, and health insurance for all ESP employees. ***He agreed to monitor Laura and Aimee's progress with Major Gifts Ramp-Up, and if they met certain financial benchmarks, he would further insure their success by investing in ESP's overhead.***

Laura and Aimee went to work implementing Major Gifts Ramp-Up's thirteen steps. Here's a brief overview of the capacity building program Carter and the Strickland Foundation underwrote on behalf of ESP:

Step #1   **Management Philosophy**   **(Planning)**

They decided that Laura was a STRONG CEO, and would continue to set aside the majority of her time to BUILD CAPACITY. They re-purposed her workflow by creating multiple weekly "task maps," based on the responsibilities outlined in the Major Gifts Ramp-Up Model.

Step #2   **Major Gifts Fundraising**   **(Planning)**

They made a decision not to be distracted by low-yield fundraising events, direct mail, or phone campaigns. They established a DONOR-DRIVEN philosophy of fundraising, ensuring that supporters and volunteers became fully integrated into ESP's mission. They determined that Major Gifts fundraising would provide the highest return, in the shortest period of time possible, at the lowest cost.

Step #3   **Organizational Development**   **(Planning)**

They audited all aspects of ESP's programs, including operations, leadership, environment, technology, and staff. Based on this information, a multi-year annual fund goal, a one-time project goal, and an endowment goal were determined. Goal amounts were based on actual needs and costs identified during the audit process.

Step #4   **Case for Support**   **(Planning)**

They believed that money "chases after ideas," and that there would always be generous people who would amply support ESP's great dream, if it was backed by a sound plan. They expressed these "ideas" and the costs to implement them in a written Case for Support document. The financials in this collateral were backed by the data gathered during the organizational development process.

Step #5   **Advancement Calendar**   **(Planning)**

They created step-by-step "task maps" containing hundreds of assignments which, when executed in order and on time, would ensure campaign success. The series of responsibilities spanned eighteen months, and were assigned to the executive director, consultant, and campaign cabinet members.

Step #6   Prospect Identification   (Cultivation)

Using the online prospect research tool, DonorScope, they downloaded complete contact information for major donors who lived within the service footprint of ESP and had a net worth of $1 million plus. They then appended publically held wealth and financial information to each family in the ESP database file. Finally, they compiled lists of known community champions who could join the campaign.

Step #7   Awareness Event   (Cultivation)

ESP then hosted a creative non-fundraising awareness event to introduce the Case for Support to newly identified campaign prospects. The purpose of this luncheon was two-fold. First, it creatively invited the "RIGHT PROSPECTS" to learn about ESP. Second, it encouraged "EXISTING SUPPORTERS" to become more involved. Over 200 of the right people attended and learned about ESP's Case for Support for the very first time.

Step #8   Prospect Cultivation   (Cultivation)

Individual Plans of Care (IPOC) were written, consisting of multiple points of contact that intentionally moved each prospect into greater involvement with ESP. Customized "Ask" objectives were determined, and each prospect was invited to join ESP in a way that worked for them.

Step #9   Signature Ask Event   (Cultivation)

The "ask event" accomplished three objectives. First, it provided an opportunity to meet more major donor prospects using the "table host" banquet model. Second, it further raised the level of visibility of ESP in the community early in the campaign. Third, it raised smaller short-term monies, allowing major donors to make a first "token" gift in advance of their later greater major gift.

Step #10   **Campaign Cabinet**   **(Solicitation)**

They now had an adequate number of fully cultivated prospects they could approach to join the campaign cabinet. These veteran fundraisers each made a significant gift and committed to giving six months of their time to making multiple solicitations, inviting their peers to join ESP's family of donors. They created a gift-range chart, and then agreed to perform five solicitations per cabinet member. The campaign cabinet determined that the top gift would be in the range of 20% of the goal. An additional ten commitments, including the first one, would be as much as 50% to 60% of goal. Finally, another 30 gifts would equal as much as 30% of goal.

Step #11   **Campaign Interviews**   **(Solicitation)**

As a result of the previous awareness event and signature ask event, the campaign cabinet was able to choose from a list of over 100 fully cultivated families who had already been introduced to ESP's Case for Support. Appointments were set by staff and cabinet members with each family, to explore how they could be financially involved in the campaign.

Step #12   **Three Part Ask**   **(Solicitation)**

During the campaign interview process, cabinet members invited each family to consider a small multi-year annual fund gift, a one-time project stretch gift, and an endowment gift through their estate plan. Because cabinet members had already made their own financial commitment and had built proper relationships with each prospect, cabinet members invited each family to make their best gift ever to this campaign.

(Please review Appendix D for an expanded overview of National Development Institute's Major Gifts Ramp-Up Model)

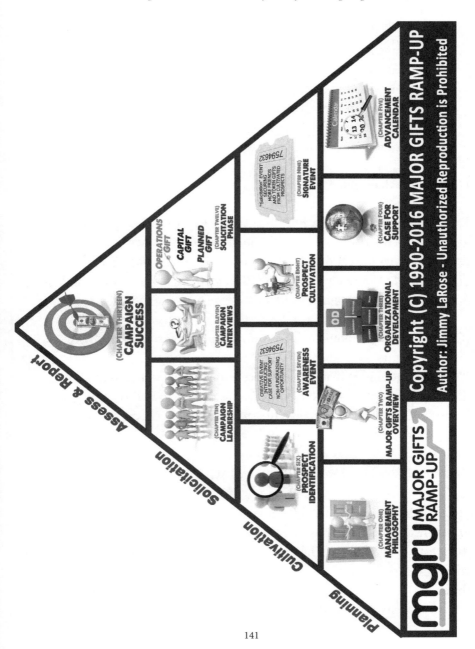

Step #13   Campaign Success   (Solicitation)

ESP's "Dream Build Campaign"...

> ...came in over goal
> ...was completed on time
> ...was executed under budget
> ...resulted in happy volunteers
> ...produce grateful donors
> ...promoted community pride

Here's where they ended up:

Laura, Aimee, Carter, Jerry, ESP's board, and generous Georgia donors gave families with developmental disabilities the gift of new facilities, expanded programs, and additional staff. ***Upon completion, ESP's "Dream Build Campaign" raised $3 Million dollars for one-time capital projects, and increased ESP's annual income to over $650,000 per year.***

(Oh...by the way...campaign success...*without a feasibility study!*)

It's important to note that Aimee Vance emphatically states, to this day, that Laura Whitaker, a STRONG CEO, was the key to ESP's campaign. Aimee insists, "If your campaign doesn't have a Laura...your campaign will fail."

Back to the Strickland Family and RE-IMAGINING PHILANTHROPY.

Here you have a group of loved ones committed to ensuring others experience life worth living. They understood that they had more to offer than just money, and that the "turnarounds" they performed for energy companies applied to nonprofit organizations as well. They understood the adage *money is oxygen* and restricted a significant portion of their gifts to capacity-building that led to greater financial sustainability. In the person of Laura Whitaker, they found a strong CEO who trusted her small board to provide support and avoid mismanagement. She believed that donors were as important as causes or people, and invested her time accordingly. She didn't demoralize her board by insisting that they fundraise, but rather had key board members serve alongside veteran volunteer fundraisers on a separate campaign cabinet that knew what they were doing. The Strickland Family supported Laura in her search for a super consultant, to ensure ESP implemented a donor-centered fundraising plan that meaningfully involved new friends. In hiring Aimee Vance, they avoided the pitfalls of outdated methods and instead implemented a model that built trust relationships with families just like the Strickland's. Both Carter and Jerry understood that "turnarounds" don't just happen, and saw Major Gifts Ramp-Up as a plan whose success was based on "intentionality." Finally, as key milestones were met, Jerry personally gave additional monies to increase salaries, secure additional support staff, and provide health care benefits for all employees.

He invested in overhead.

These "big ideas" revealed themselves over a period of weeks and months because Laura committed to building capacity. She went ahead and:

1. Attended a MAJOR GIFTS RAMP-UP CONFERENCE
2. Purchased the MAJOR GIFTS RAMP-UP CLOUD
3. Launched a MAJOR GIFTS RAMP-UP CAMPAIGN

It reminds me of something Thomas Jefferson once said, *"The harder I work the luckier I seem to get!"*

As they say on the evening shows…GOOD NIGHT EVERYBODY!!!

RIP QUIZ #7

1. Please respond to the following statement: "Jerry Strickland gave restricted gifts to overhead!"

2. Please respond to the following statement: "Smart donors invest in both programs AND capacity-building."

3. Do you serve a nonprofit that needs to implement Major Gifts Ramp-Up? If your answer is yes, explain why. If your answer is no, explain why.

4. Respond to this statement: "Laura Whitaker was the key to ESP's fundraising success!"

IN CONCLUSION

I think the reason why I don't read so much is because, as I have observed, whole books all boil down to a drop of essence. You can read a book full of ten thousand words and, at the end, sum it up in one sentence; I am more for the one sentence. I am more for the essence.

~C. JoyBell C.

RE-IMAGINING PHILANTHROPY in one sentence is:

GIVE DIFFERENTLY.

A noted author once wrote, *"The only difference between writers and people who don't write is that writers aren't afraid to display their demons."*

With that quote in mind, I might as well have titled this book, *CONFESSIONS OF A TEENAGE FUNDRAISING CONSULTANT*, for in my youth, I was complicit in the selling of status quo products and services that never should have been offered in the first place.

Granted, it took years to recognize that our industry leaders were stuck in the past. Once I discerned that the concepts being bandied about were ineffective, my repentance came quickly. Albeit too late for one nonprofit, to whom I sold a feasibility study with the full knowledge of what the outcome would be ("YOU'RE NOT READY."). The remorse that followed drove me into a decade long journey to sort out the problems, and replace them with solutions that worked.

I spent years researching, gathering data, and testing ideas, only to discover, in the end, that what I really needed was…

…YOU!!!

As I noted earlier, as a philanthropist, you are in the unique position to use your monies, acumen, abilities, and wisdom to solve multi-billion dollar problems of scale. We'll do this through a brand new re-tooled charitable sector that you've transformed and clothed in immense power.

You have the authority to make this happen. You have the power to make this happen faster. All you have to do is...GIVE DIFFERENTLY.

Let's do it together.

Finally, and in closing, I'm reminded of the warning you see so often on television that goes something like this...

...DO NOT TRY THIS AT HOME!

Implementing the big ideas found in this book will decimate most nonprofit organizations (yes...some need to be decimated).

Regardless, RE-IMAGINING PHILANTHROPY is not a broad-sword to be wielded with violence, but rather a scalpel to be carefully used, to heal organizations in different stages of health and need. Let me encourage you to find a like-minded professional who can bring the best of your world to the nonprofits you love and support. None of this is rocket-science, but a little bit of nuance can go a long way to ensure your goals are more easily met.

I look forward to meeting you personally. Feel free to give me a ring at the offices of National Development Institute at 800-257-6670.

Until then, I Remain, Sincerely Yours,

Jimmy LaRose

jimmy@jimmylarose.com

To learn more about Jimmy and the organizations he promotes and oversees please visit:

www.NANOE.org
www.facebook.com/NANOEmembers
www.twitter.com/NANOEcentral
www.JimmyLaRose.com
www.twitter.com/jimmylarose
www.MajorGiftsRampUp.com
www.NonprofitConferences.org
www.Development.net
www.PAXglobal.com
www.DonorScope.com
www.501c3.buzz
www.WhoCaresTV.com

National Development Institute
P.O Box 1840 - Lexington, SC 29071
Voice: 803-808-5084 Fax: 803-808-0537
jimmy@jimmylarose.com

APPENDIX A – SAMPLE ORGANIZATIONAL CHARTS

Traditional Board Organizational Chart (15 Members)

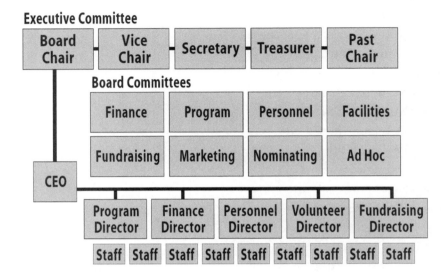

Better Board Organizational Chart (5 Members)

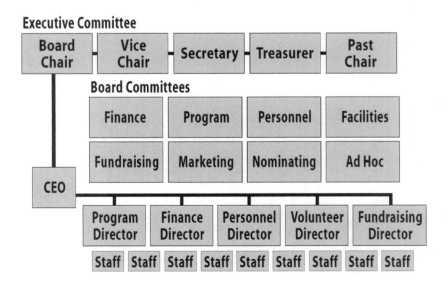

United Way Organizational Chart (25 Members)

Executive Committee

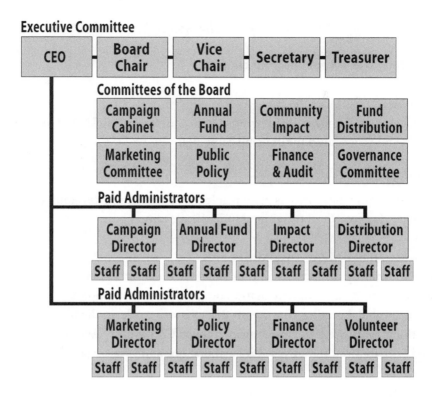

APPENDIX B - UNITED WAY COMMITTEE DESCRIPTIONS

Governance functions are highlighted ***BOLD, ITALIC and UNDERLINE.***

Everything else is a volunteer function.

CAMPAIGN COMMITTEE
The Campaign Committee is responsible for implementing United Way's annual and year-round fundraising campaign.

ANNUAL FUND COMMITTEE
The Campaign Committee is responsible for planning and developing strategies for growth of the annual fundraising campaign.

COMMUNITY IMPACT COMMITTEE
The Community Impact Committee leads the organization in the transition to and implementation of the Community Impact organizational direction. The committee oversees works in the four functional work areas of Community Impact: Community Assessment, Fund Distribution, Initiatives and Partnerships, and Programs.

FUND DISTRIBUTION COMMITTEE
United Way's Fund Distribution process requires Volunteer Panelists to review and evaluate affiliated agency requests for United Way program funding. Each panel is comprised of a broad representation of the community. United Way's Fund Distribution process engages community members in the decision making process of where United Way funds will be invested.

MARKETING COMMITTEE
The marketing committee is responsible for planning, coordinating, and implementing marketing strategies and communications programs that educate and involve selected audiences as well as the general community in supporting the United Way mission and strategies.

PUBLIC POLICY COMMITTEE
Proposes, analyzes, supports and influences public policies, at all levels of government, that support our community impact agenda and accomplish our missional goals.

GOVERNANCE COMMITTEE
The governance committee is responsible for developing and supporting actions that cultivate new and existing Board Members including _**nominations of new members.**_

**FINANCE COMMITTEE**
**The Finance Committee is responsible for providing financial oversight for the organization including review of the annual audit.**

**EXECUTIVE COMMITTEE**
**Executive Committee is comprised of officers and evaluates the performance of the executive director, sets the Board agenda, reviews the by-laws and recommends changes as necessary.**

MAJOR GIFTS RAMP-UP MOTIVATION MATRIX (redux)

TYPE	CAUSE	REQUIREMENTS	PERSONALITY	COMMUNICA'
• Communitarian	• Religion	• Shared Values/Mission	• Extraversion	• One-On-One
• Devout	• Education	• Financially Stable	• Introversion	• Phone/Mobile
• Investors	• Human Welfare	• Interest in Project	• Sensing	• Email/Online
• Socialite	• Healthcare	• Staff Leadership	• Intuition	• Social Media
• Repayer	• Public Benefit	• Volunteer Leadership	• Thinking	• Onsite/Tour
• Altruist	• Arts/Culture	• Respected Locally	• Feeling	• Direct Mail
• Dynast	• International	• Respected Nationally	• Judging	• Special Events
	• Environment	• Influence of Solicitor	• Perceiving	• Video/Streamii
(Seven Faces of Philanthropy)	• Animals	• Memorial Opportunity		• Collateral Doc
		• Gift Recognition	*(Myers-Briggs)*	
		• Challenge Gift		
		• Campaign Cabinet		
		• Board/Committee Service		

MAJOR GIFTS RAMP-UP MOTIVATION MATRIX (expanded)

WHAT TYPE ARE YOU? *(Seven Faces of Philanthropy)*

- Communitarian   (26%)   "Doing Good Makes Good Sense"
- Devout   (21%)   "Doing Good is God's Will"
- Investors   (15%)   "Doing Good is Good Business"
- Socialite   (11%)   "Doing Good is Fun"
- Repayer   (10%)   "Doing Good in Return"
- Altruist   (9%)   "Doing Good Feels Right"
- Dynast   (8%)   "Doing Good is a Family Tradition"

WHAT CAUSES DO YOU CARE ABOUT?

• Religion	(31%)	• Arts/Culture	(5%)
• Education	(16%)	• International	(4%)
• Human Welfare	(12%)	• Environment	(3%)
• Healthcare	(10%)	• Animals	(1%)
• Public Benefit	(7%)		

MAJOR GIFTS RAMP-UP MOTIVATION MATRIX (cont.)

WHAT DO YOU REQUIRE FROM A NONPROFIT?

- Shared Values/Mission
- Financially Stable
- Interest in Project
- Staff Leadership
- Volunteer Leadership
- Respected Locally
- Respected Nationally
- Influence of Solicitor
- Memorial Opportunity
- Gift Recognition
- Challenge/Leadership Gift
- Campaign Cabinet
- Board/Committee Service

YOUR PERSONALITY:

- Extraversion (E)
- Introversion (I)
- Sensing (S)
- Intuition (N)
- Thinking (T)
- Feeling (F)
- Judging (J)
- Perceiving (P)

Favorite world: Do you prefer to focus on the outer world, or on your own inner world? Extraversion (E) vs. Introversion (I). ***Information:*** Do you prefer to focus on the basic information you take in, or do you prefer to interpret and add meaning? Sensing (S) vs. Intuition (N). ***Decisions:*** When making decisions, do you prefer to first look at logic and consistency, or first look at the people and special circumstances? Thinking (T) vs. Feeling (F). ***Structure:*** In dealing with the outside world, do you prefer to get things decided, or do you prefer to stay open to new information and options? Judging (J) vs. Perceiving (P).

HOW DO YOU PREFER TO TRANSACT?

- One-On-One
- Phone/Mobile
- Social Media
- Direct Mail
- Special Events
- Collateral Documents
- Email/Online
- Video/Streaming

APPENDIX D – Major Gifts Ramp-Up Model – How Laura, Aimee, Carter, Jerry, and Extra Special People exceeded a $3,000,000 fundraising goal and increased annual fund by 220%

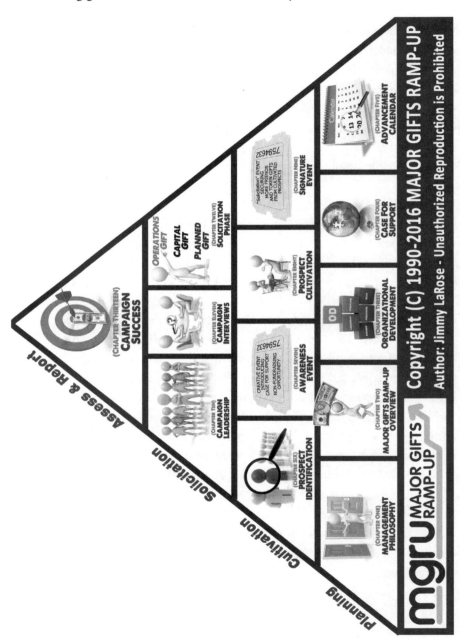

I. CAMPAIGN DIAGNOSTIC – PREPARING TO PLAN

In order to properly prepare for Major Gifts Ramp-Up, ESP will first need to complete National Development Institute's (NDI) Comprehensive Campaign Diagnostic (CCD). The CCD is a confidential detailed assessment of your nonprofit that will assist our team as we lay a foundation for future expansion in development. The CCD is divided into eight sections. They are as follows:

1. Basic Institutional Data
2. Programs/Services
3. Staff/Administration/Volunteers
4. Heritage/History
5. Income/Disbursements/Finances
6. Fund Raising/Development
7. Polity/Governance
8. Upcoming Projects/Conclusion

Upon completion of the CCD, ESP will provide existing documentation regarding the following areas of organizational development.

1. Administrative personnel and support staff
2. Board and committee structures
3. Volunteer/advocacy/leadership programs
4. Established linkages to constituencies
5. Program, fundraising & marketing calendars
6. Annual fund, capital project & estate planning marketing materials
7. Architectural drawings, renderings, designs & blue prints
8. Marketing collaterals and website platforms
9. Donor cultivation management systems
10. Gift acceptance policies
11. Donor records and fundraising reports
12. Written strategic plans
13. Written fundraising plans

II. SCOPE OF SERVICE – RAISING MAJOR GIFTS

Step #1 – Management Philosophy

ESP leadership and your NDI counselors will determine who will **execute** the approved campaign plan and (as a separate matter) determine what group of administrators will take responsibility to **monitor** the execution of the plan on a daily/weekly/monthly basis.

(Tasks will be equally shared between your NDI Counselor, ESP Administrators, and various board committee chairs)

Step #2 – Major Gifts Ramp-Up Overview

The team will identify key leaders who represent different levels of sponsorship who should be cultivated, engaged and oriented to the proposed campaign plan. This step will ensure that the organization as a whole is unified around this new initiative.

Written cultivation plans ensuring the development of internal sponsors could include:

a) <u>Initiating Sponsors</u> – Who are the trusted and competent leaders who will oversee this project, bringing credibility to the campaign?

b) <u>Executive Sponsors</u> – All senior administrators must be knowledgeable and openly supportive of the campaign.

c) <u>Sustaining Sponsors</u> – What program or department heads must be fully briefed on the campaign? What is their role in supporting the campaign and how could this change any of their current responsibilities?

(This task will be performed by NDI Counselor supported by ESP Personnel)

Step #3 – Organizational Development

Every nonprofit is broadly comprised of Leadership, Operations, Staff, Environment & Technology. These dimensions will be inventoried and the needs/costs of each will be identified to determine a proper funding/project/campaign goal. The team will work with relevant administrators *to conduct an Organizational Readiness Review.*

(This task will be overseen by your NDI Counselor but will primarily be the responsibility of ESP Personnel)

Step #4 – Case for Support

Making the case is the quintessential development task for any nonprofit. The process of determining Case for Support elements must reflect the unified vision of all the individuals responsible for organizational stewardship. Campaign timelines and budgets for campaign expenses and income will be identified and included with the campaign collateral materials that are developed during this phase.

a) Categorize separate sets of services/programs unique to organization
b) Determine separate project/operational expansion goals
c) Formulate associated dollar amounts for each expansion goal
d) Write a campaign timeline with campaign completion dates

(The gathering of existing case copy elements will be the responsibility of ESP with NDI Counselor oversight. Your NDI Counselor will adjust and finalize copy. Graphic design and printing of the case document will be the responsibility of ESP Personnel)

Step #5 – Advancement Calendar

Key team members will create step-by-step "task maps" containing numerous assignments which, when executed in order and on time, will ensure campaign success. These could include but will not be limited to:

a) scheduled trustees/board meetings
b) existing program events
c) print/copy/artwork due dates
d) non-fundraising awareness events
e) signature "ask" events

(This task will be performed by NDI Counselor supported by ESP Personnel)

Step #6 – Prospect Identification

Using the online prospect research tool, DonorScope, the team will first download complete contact information of major donors whose net worth exceeds $1,000,000 who live within the service footprint of your nonprofit. Second, the team will add comprehensive wealth & financial information to each person or family in their existing database file. Third, the team will create lists of known community champions, board members and major donors who could join your nonprofit by sharing a major gift. The final step will be to record the first and last name of each prospect and then cross-reference this information against both the secured lists and internal file. If an address record cannot be located, Google, Internet White Pages, and other online resources will be used to secure complete contact information.

(This task will be overseen by your NDI Counselor but will primarily be the responsibility of ESP Personnel)

Step #7 – Awareness Events

A non-fundraising awareness event will be held to publically introduce the Case for Support to identified campaign prospects. An Awareness Event is a uniquely creative breakfast or lunch meeting that highlights a nonprofit's mission and compelling Case for Support. The purpose of an Awareness Event is two-fold. First, it creatively invites the "RIGHT PROSPECTS" to learn about your mission. Second, it encourages your "EXISTING SUPPORTERS" to become more meaningfully involved. Quite often, an Awareness Event will be the first time community champions, foundation executives, corporate leaders, or individuals of wealth and influence are introduced to the newly created Case for Support. This event will be the first significant point of contact followed by a series of cultivation "Touch-Points" that will result in earning the right to ask for a financial investment.

(Responsibility will be shared between NDI Counselor and ESP Personnel)

Step #8 – Prospect Cultivation

Cultivation strategies will be created that intentionally move each prospect into greater involvement with the organization. "Ask" objectives will be determined (see list below) and then supported by written Individual Plans of Care (IPOC) for each prospect. There are a variety of venues, vehicles, and methods that can be employed as touch points (see list below) when writing a prospect's individual plan of care.

"Ask" Objectives:

a) Board Members
b) Committee Members
c) Campaign Cabinet Members
d) Campaign Visitors
e) Foundation Givers

f) Corporate Underwriters
g) Major Donors
h) Legacy Givers
i) Local Church Advocates
j) Performance Volunteers
k) Event Table Hosts

(This task will be overseen by your NDI Counselor but will primarily be the responsibility of ESP Personnel)

Step #9 – Signature "Ask" Event

The Signature "Ask" Event model will be deployed to both cultivate major donor prospects and raise smaller amounts of money in the short term. The Signature "Ask" event provides first time major donor prospects the opportunity to make their first "token" gift in advance of their participation in campaign interviews.

(This task will be overseen by your NDI Counselor but will primarily be the responsibility of ESP Personnel)

Step #10 – Volunteer Campaign Leadership

Campaign Cabinet Members will emerge from the cultivation process. These volunteers are responsible to make the "ask" and to invite their peers to join the campaign and match their personal financial investment. Campaign Leadership's confidence is dramatically increased when they are included in the following decision-making processes.

a) How many gifts and what specific dollar amounts have to be raised?
b) Who is going to be asked and for how much?
c) Who is going to do the asking?
d) What is the timeline to reach campaign goal?

Step #11 – Campaign Interviews

One of the most crucial elements of success in this process will be the identification and solicitation of top gifts. Statistical analysis suggests that the top gift will be in the range of 20% of the goal. The top ten commitments, including the first one, will be as much as 50% to 60% of the goal or success is in jeopardy. Another 30 gifts will usually equal as much as 30%. Interview processes will be developed by the Campaign Cabinet and will include:

a) Campaign Interview Task Map Creation
b) Orientation & Internal Information Gathering
c) Survey Questionnaire Development
d) Collateral Document Development
e) Identification of Potential Donor Prospects
f) Campaign Interviews via personal visits, focus groups, direct mail
g) Data Compilation & Information Analysis
h) Presentation of Cultivation Report & Recommendations

(Responsibility for this task will fall primarily on the shoulders of your NDI Counselor but will require considerable support by ESP Personnel)

Step #12 – Solicitation Phase

The strongest volunteers will be trained in how to make the "three- part ask" including multi-year operational commitments, one-time project investment, and endowment gift. It may be necessary to use staff, administration, or board members to make solicitations though the ideal presentation should include a volunteer (already in relationship) who can look their friend in the eye and invite them to give the big gift.
Each campaign visitor will be equipped with a very specific set of collateral documents (customized per campaign initiative) that keep a visitor on message and provide them the confidence they need to "ask."

These documents generally include:

a) Detailed Proposal
b) Gift Commitment Agreement
c) Case for Support Document

(Responsibility will be shared between your NDI Counselor and ESP Personnel)

Step #13 – Campaign Success

The success of these initiatives will be determined by the following metrics:

a) Exceeding the pre-determined fundraising goal
b) Completing the project on schedule
c) Coming in under campaign budget
d) Fostering community pride
e) Celebrating volunteers who are happy they participated
f) Thanking donors who are grateful they invested

III. MAJOR GIFTS RAMP-UP CLOUD

ESP will be provided a lifetime subscription to the Major Gifts Ramp-Up Cloud to support the implementation of this ongoing initiative. Recognized as the world's largest nonprofit digital resource library, the MGRU Cloud includes over 10,000 pages of documents, tutorials, presentations, manuals, videos, audios, curriculum and exams vital to enhancing your organization's performance. Team members will save a tremendous amount of time as they CUT-AND-PASTE their way through hundreds of projects using fresh material they own.

To learn more about Jimmy LaRose please visit:

www.NANOE.org
www.facebook.com/NANOEmembers
www.twitter.com/NANOEcentral
www.JimmyLaRose.com
www.twitter.com/jimmylarose
www.MajorGiftsRampUp.com
www.NonprofitConferences.org
www.Development.net
www.PAXglobal.com
www.DonorScope.com
www.501c3.buzz
www.WhoCaresTV.com

National Development Institute
P.O Box 1840 - Lexington, SC 29071
Voice: 803-808-5084 Fax: 803-808-0537
jimmy@jimmylarose.com

BIBLIOGRAPHY

Association of Fundraising Professionals *"Association of Fundraising Professionals Standards"* Adopted 1964; amended Oct. 2014 Standards

Burns, Michael *"The CEO as Board Chair"* Nonprofit Quarterly, 2013, Article

Carver, John *"Boards That Make a Difference"* Jossey-Bass, 1997, Book

Chait, Richard P., Holland, Thomas P., and Taylor, Barbara E. *"Improving the Performance of Governing Board"* American Council on Education and The Oryx Press, 1996, Book

Collins, Jim *"Good to Great and the Social Sectors: A Monograph to Accompany Good to Great"* Harper Business, 2005, Book

Delaney, Thomas *"Everybody wants to go to heaven, but nobody wants to die"* Tom (Thomas Henry) Delaney (1889-1963) Song

Drucker, Peter F. *Management: Tasks, Responsibilities, Practices.* Harper Collins, 1974, Book

Frantzreb, Arthur *Feasibility Studies: Probability? or Productivity!* Hartsook Companies, 1998, Monograph

Geneen, Harold S. *"Why Directors Can't Protect the Shareholders"* Fortune, 1984, Book

Gillies, James *"Boardroom Renaissance"* McGraw-Hill Ryerson and The National Centre for Management Research and Development, 1992, Book

Giving Institute *"Statement of Best Practices Adopted By Giving Institute Member Firms"* Amended 2015 Standards

Goldstein, Henry *"Fundraising Consultants Need to Debunk Misconceptions About Feasibility Studies"* The Chronicle of Philanthropy, 2015, Article

Hall, Holly *"Author Says Feasibility Studies for Capital Campaigns Are a Waste"* The Chronicle of Philanthropy, 2015, Article

LaRose, Jimmy *"Major Gifts Ramp-Up: The Effectual Dynamics of Resource Development"* National Development Institute, 2010, Book

Light, Paul *"Sustaining Nonprofit Performance: The Case for Capacity Building and the Evidence to Support It"* Brookings Institution Press, 2004, Book

Myers, Peter B., Myers, Isabel Briggs *"Gifts Differing: Understanding Personality Type"* CPP; Reprint edition, 1995

Pallotta, Dan *"The way we think about charity is dead wrong"* Ted Talk, 2009, Video

Panas, Jerold *"MegaGifts: Who Gives Them, Who Gets Them"* Pluribus Press, 1984, Book

Robinson, Kathleen, LaRose, Jimmy *"Nonprofit Capacity Building in a Post-Recession Economy"*, National Development Institute, 2013, White Paper

Prince, Russ Alan, File, Karen Maru *"The Seven Faces of Philanthropy: A New Approach to Cultivating Major Donors"* 2001, Jossey-Bass Pfeiffer, Book